Learning the Git Bash Shell

Become a Windows Command Line Commando

Version 1.01

Michael Hanna

Copyright

Cover Photo

Disclaimer

While I have tried to provide information that is accurate to the best of my knowledge, I cannot accept any liability for consequential damages for use of the information in this book. If typos, bugs in the software or your misuse of the software results in the launch of nuclear weapons, crashes of cars or aircraft, nationwide power outages, asteroid impacts, Biblical floods, plagues of locusts, traffic jams, or Distributed Denial of Service attacks from bored teenagers, that is your problem, not mine. Deal with it. ☺

Table of Contents

Introduction _____ 1
Who This Book is For _____ 2
What This Book is Not _____ 2
Formatting Notes _____ 3
Overview and Motivation _____ 5
What is Git and Version Control? _____ 5
What is the Git Bash Shell? _____ 6
Why Use Git Bash Instead of Cygwin or a Virtual Machine? _____ 7
Git Bash + Your Favorite Editor is Better and Leaner Than An IDE ___ 9
How to Download and Install msysgit for Windows _____ 11
Configuring the Git Bash Shortcut _____ 23
Copying and Pasting to/from the Git Bash Shell Window _____ 23
Alternate Consoles for Git Bash _____ 27
Basic Bash _____ 29
A Note on Directories and How Git Bash Handles Windows Drive Names ___ 30
How to Handle File and Path Names with Spaces _____ 30
Built-in Commands _____ 31
  Directory Handling Commands _____ 34
  Command Line Completion _____ 36
  Bash Command History _____ 37
  Job Control with Foreground and Background Jobs _____ 42
  Other Shell Builtins _____ 45
External Commands _____ 46
Arguments to Commands _____ 47
  Hidden Files _____ 47
More About Command Arguments _____ 48
GNU Utilities: The Hidden Bonus of the Git Bash Shell _____ 49
  Where are These Utilities Really Located? _____ 50
Shell File Globbing _____ 54
  How to Find Things _____ 65
Regular Expressions and grep _____ 70
  Useful Options for grep _____ 79
I/O Redirection and Pipes _____ 80
Bash Variables _____ 86
  Predefined Variables and Positional Parameters _____ 86
  The shift Builtin _____ 91
  Prompt Variables _____ 92

Local Versus Global Variables_____93
Using env and set to Look at Global and Local Variables_____95
Using set and shopt to Set and Unset Shell Options_____97
*The Power of Aliases*_____100
*The Power of Shell Functions*_____102
*Subshells*_____102
*Other Shells*_____104
*Command Substitution*_____105
*Configuring Bash with the .bashrc File*_____106
Where is the .bashrc File?_____106
Editing and Sourcing the .bashrc File_____107
The Critical Importance of Setting the Proper $PATH Variable_____107
Storing Variables, Aliases and Shell Functions in .bashrc_____109
More Advanced Bash_____111
*The Bash Programming Language*_____111
*Writing Scripts*_____111
*If-Then-Else Statements*_____112
*Case Statements*_____115
*Testing Conditions*_____116
*For Loops*_____118
*Break and Continue Statements*_____122
*While Loops*_____125
Redirecting I/O for Loops_____132
*Until Loops*_____133
Using Your Favorite Editor from Git Bash_____135
*Vim and GVim*_____136
*Emacs*_____142
*Notepad++*_____146
*Sublime Text 2*_____152
Using Ruby from Git Bash_____159
Using Python from Git Bash_____161
Using the XAMPP LAMP Stack from Git Bash_____163
GNU on Windows: More Goodies You Can Run from Bash_____165
GnuWin: Even More Utilities You Can Run from Bash_____171
Miscellaneous Utilities Like jq for Reading JSON Files_____173
Basic Git_____175
*Configuring Global Commands*_____176
*Initializing a Repository*_____176
*Adding Files to the Staging Area/Index*_____178
*Committing Files*_____179

*Setting a Default Editor*_____**180**
   Setting Notepad++ as the Default Editor_____**181**
   Setting Sublime Text 2 as the Default Editor_____**181**
*Creating a Label*_____**182**
*Looking at Information in the Repository*_____**182**
*Basic Branching*_____**185**
*Basic Merging*_____**187**
*Git: Attack of the Clones*_____**192**
*Setting Up a Remote Repository for Collaborating with Others*_____**195**
*Pushing to and Pulling from Remote Repositories*_____**198**
Using SSH to Connect to Remote Repositories_____**203**
*Creating SSH Keys*_____**204**
*Creating an SSH Configuration File*_____**205**
*Installing the Public Key into Bitbucket*_____**205**
*Testing the Connection*_____**207**
*Configuring Bitbucket to Use SSH Instead of HTTPS*_____**208**
*Connecting to a Remote Repository Via SSH*_____**209**
*Eliminating Most Passphrases by Running ssh-agent*_____**213**
Conclusion_____**223**
Appendix_____**225**
*Bash Reference Books*_____**225**
*Git Reference Books*_____**225**
*Bash Online References*_____**225**
*Git Online References*_____**226**
Acknowledgments_____**229**
Index_____**231**

Introduction

Welcome to the Git Bash shell, the most powerful Windows command line environment that you never heard of! While any recent version of Windows provides an elegant Graphical User Interface (or GUI) that makes many common tasks easy to do, experienced software developers – who need to do a much more complex variety of tasks than the average computer user – know that it is often much more efficient to work directly in a command line environment. This is partly because software developers need to get 'under the hood' of the machine to design and run programs, and connect them efficiently to various parts of the local operating system as well as to the Internet as a whole. It is also partly because not every tool that developers need to use has a convenient GUI available. And some tools just don't work well graphically. But the most important reason to work in a command line environment is speed and efficiency.

To younger developers who have grown up never knowing anything but beautiful graphical interfaces (whether they be Macintosh or Windows), it may seem counter-intuitive that the command line should be preferred over an elegant GUI. As you gain experience, you will find that there are many situations where using the command line is much faster than attempting to use a GUI, and some situations where the command line is your only option. (Need to log in regularly to large numbers of remote machines using the SSH protocol? You won't find this very enjoyable from a GUI, if you can do it at all.)

Unfortunately, Microsoft has never shown much interest in making it easy to work from the command line. The default command-line environment in Windows is invoked by running cmd.exe, more commonly known as a 'DOS box' due to it being legacy DOS software that has been incorporated into Windows for backward compatibility. This provides a very primitive environment that accepts commands from the user, but doesn't make it easy to do very much with them.

The advent of Windows PowerShell provided much better capabilities, but in addition to having its own set of idiosyncrasies, it is only available on the Windows platform. While PowerShell can certainly interface with Linux systems, most people who do Web development need to work directly on UNIX- or Linux-based systems at least some of the time. This is because most of the world's Web servers run some variant of UNIX or Linux rather than Windows. Thus it is very handy for Web developers to be able to work directly in a UNIX-like environment, even when working on a Windows machine. (Note that while there are historical, legal, and architectural differences between UNIX and Linux, they are similar enough to each other that we will use the terms largely interchangeably during the course of this book. Some people favor using the more general term "*nix" to refer to any of the huge number of UNIX and Linux variants. Although UNIX and Linux have different kernel architectures, system administration tools, and file systems, with respect to the tools that software developers use on a daily basis, Linux can be regarded largely as a superset of UNIX. All of the traditional UNIX tools work fine on Linux, but on Linux most of these tools have additional options and capabilities. Linux systems also have many additional tools that didn't exist on UNIX systems.)

Who This Book is For

This book is for software developers, students, and hobbyists who wish to do their development work in a UNIX-style environment on a Windows machine without having to deal with the additional overhead and configuration headaches of running a Linux virtual machine. It is also for people who are interested in learning the basics of how UNIX and its descendent Linux works, without having to install a full Linux environment or set up a dual-boot machine. Finally, and perhaps most importantly, this book is for people who have spent their lives using graphical user interfaces and thus may have an innate fear of command lines. Instead of fearing the command line, my goal is to teach you to be a Command Line Commando!

What This Book is Not

Perhaps somewhat surprisingly, this is not a book about Git or even primarily the Bash shell, though we will cover some of the rudiments of each (especially Bash). Rather, it is about how to properly install Git, and how to configure the Bash shell for use with many of your favorite applications. It is also a tutorial on using some of the many utilities that are installed along with Git and Bash.

The Git Bash shell can be used with your favorite editor and your favorite programming languages. It can even be used with a complete development environment like XAMPP, one of the many so-called LAMP stacks that is commonly used for Web development. (LAMP is an acronym for "Linux Apache MySQL and PHP," a set of tools that make Web development much easier.) Do you prefer to use Ruby on Rails or Python and Django? Or perhaps some other language/framework combination? Chances are that you can use your favorite tools directly from the Git Bash shell, by following the guidelines in this book.

Formatting Notes

Computer code is displayed in the monospace DejaVu Sans Mono font. Complete scripts are displayed with a box around them.

I should also note that I have followed the tradition of starting new chapters on right-hand (odd-numbered) pages. This means that a blank page needs to be inserted if the previous chapter ends on an odd-numbered page. So don't be concerned about blank left-hand pages - like the one that follows this one.

Now let's get started.

Overview and Motivation

Let's get started with a brief discussion of what Git and Bash are, and why you might want to use them. They are really two conceptually separate pieces of software, even though they are bundled into a single application.

For the record, this book uses Git version 1.9.0-preview20140217 running on a Windows 7 Home Premium 64-bit system with 4 GB of RAM.

What is Git and Version Control?

Git is one of the most popular version control systems. It was invented by Linus Torvalds (the founder of Linux) to aid him in doing modifications to the Linux kernel. Although Linux is based on UNIX, the source code was developed separately to avoid legal and licensing issues. It is an open source project with thousands of contributors all over the world. These thousands of people all need to keep track of every change they make to the Linux source code.

Large projects like this can involve thousands or even tens of thousands of source files. In a real-world project like this, it is very easy for developers to accidentally (or maliciously) delete source files. Version control systems help protect against accidents like this by copying each source file into a database (of sorts) called a **repository**. More importantly, they keep track of each **version** of a source file, tracking every change from the start of a project to its end, along with additional data about who made each change and when, and a description of the reason for the change. This makes it much easier to track down problems when they occur.

A single application can be comprised of many files. A version control system can also apply a **label** (including a release number) to the complete set of files associated with one application. A new application might have labels like 'V1.0' and 'V1.1' if there has only been one significant upgrade to the software since its release. If a critical problem is discovered in V1.1 of the software, it is easy to retrieve V1.0 and use the older version instead until the newer release can be fixed.

Many older revision control systems (such as RCS and CVS) require that each developer submit all changes to a **master repository.** Having a centralized repository makes good conceptual sense, but is in practice somewhat risky. The repository must be backed up regularly if it is not to be vulnerable to things like hard disk failures, accidents by system administrators, or infiltration by hackers. Git improves on this model by using a **decentralized** architecture. Each user gets a complete copy of the repository. While it is still common in most projects to have one copy of the repository designated as the master, the presence of numerous other copies of the data help ensure that the full repository can be recovered even in the event of a disaster. (This architecture does, however, depend on the developers regularly updating the master repository – and ultimately each others' repositories – with their changes. It is still possible to lose data if a repository with unique data is destroyed before it can be copied elsewhere. But the odds of losing a significant amount of data are very low if the developers make a habit of updating the master repository regularly.)

Git is a very powerful tool and one well worth learning even by hobbyists, since version control is a vital part of every open source project as well as every professional project. However, because Git is a tool very thoroughly based on the philosophy of Linux, it has numerous options and a steep learning curve (even though learning the basics is pretty easy).

If you are someone who is just starting off in Web development, you may prefer to defer learning a version control application until after you get more experience with the actual programming needed to create a Web application. The good news is you can use the Git Bash shell without having to know Git at all!

What is the Git Bash Shell?

The Git Bash shell provides a command-line interpreter that runs an emulation of the Linux Bash shell directly under any modern version of Windows. Each instance of invoking Git Bash (by double-clicking on the Git Bash icon on your desktop) gives you a window that looks much like a traditional Windows DOS box. You will see a prompt (a dollar sign '$' by default). You simply type in commands at the prompt and then press the <Enter> key to execute them. This can work very similarly to a DOS box for simple tasks. For example, to get a listing of the files in the current directory from a DOS box, you would simply type

```
> dir
```

The same command in a Git Bash window would be

```
$ ls
```

(In each example above, the first character shown is the prompt; '>' in the case of a DOS box, and '$' in the case of Bash. **Do not** type the prompt when entering a command; just type 'dir' or 'ls' followed by hitting the <Enter> key.)

As you learn to do more complex tasks, you will find that you not only have many more commands available in Bash, but you can perform many more sophisticated operations with them as well.

The concept of a shell originated with the UNIX operating system. A shell is a command-line interpreter. It waits for you to type a command and then executes it. Under UNIX and Linux, a shell is much more powerful than this. The shell actually supports an entire programming language, You can directly type instructions in at the prompt, or run a file full of commands as a separate application, called a **shell script.** This allows you to not only mix and match existing commands, but also lets you create new ones as needed. The UNIX philosophy is that each command should do one task well, and that more sophisticated tasks should be performed by combining simpler commands. One interesting historical aspect of UNIX is that multiple shells were invented, each having their own programming language and slightly different features and syntax. You could run any of these shells at any time, which was very flexible.

Even Windows has followed this model. You can run a traditional DOS box or the newer Windows PowerShell. This flexibility made it possible for the Git Bash shell and similar third-party tools to be developed to run on Windows.

Why Use Git Bash Instead of Cygwin or a Virtual Machine?

Cygwin is an open source application that provides a more complete Linux-style environment under Windows. It not only includes more utilities, it also includes the entire X Window System for running graphical applications. Some people like using it, but the more complete environment also means more conflicts with Windows, since the architecture of Windows and UNIX systems are very different.

For example, there can be problems due to the two systems having different conventions for line endings in text files. UNIX and Linux use linefeeds (also known as newline characters), and Windows systems use a carriage return followed by a linefeed.

Cygwin has a reputation for being rather slow and hogs a lot more disk space, which isn't too surprising considering that it contains more functionality than the Git Bash shell. It is also more involved to install and configure. The type of questions you need to ask yourself are: Do I need all this extra capability? Do I really need a full-blown X Windows display server when Windows already provides a perfectly good GUI? In my experience, the answer is a resounding "NO." The Git Bash environment is modest in size and provides good performance. And it has enough familiar utilities that you can set up a productive workflow in much the same way you could on any UNIX or Linux system.

If you really need all the capabilities that Cygwin has to offer, you might as well consider taking the next step up, and simply install an entire Linux system running as a virtual machine. This is relatively easy to do using products like VirtualBox or VMWare, but most developers need more than a stock bare-bones Linux system. If you take this route, you'll be responsible for setting up and configuring an entire Linux system. This can be a rather involved task if you are new to Linux and/or you have limited system administration skills. Surprisingly, most Linux distributions don't include many of the software tools commonly used by developers. Even popular programmers' editors like gVim and emacs have to be installed by hand. Want half a dozen of your favorite programming languages? They probably aren't installed by default and you'll have to get them yourself. Need MySQL or a Web server? Depending on the distribution, you may have to set those up yourself as well.

Virtual machines have a reputation for being slow, which makes perfect sense when you realize that virtual machines impose many additional layers of complexity on top of an already complex system. The processors on newer machines now provide some hardware support for virtualization. This helps, but a virtual machine is still never going to be as fast as the host system.

Virtual machines have other issues as well, involving communicating with the host machine. In VirtualBox, for example, you have to install an extra library if you want to be able to cut and paste between your Windows host and the virtual machine. (On the other hand, you can cut and paste directly between any Git Bash window and any other Windows application.) For any virtual machine, you will also likely need to do some network configuration and firewall configuration.

The good news is that a virtual machine can provide a completely isolated 'sandbox' in which you can test applications without fear of disrupting the host system in any way. But if you don't need infrastructure with this degree of sophistication, Git Bash is much simpler.

Git Bash + Your Favorite Editor is Better and Leaner Than An IDE

Many developers are fond of using an Integrated Development Environment (IDE), such as Eclipse or NetBeans. You can certainly use such tools in conjunction with the Git Bash shell if you want to, but my question to you is, why bother? While an IDE will often provide an elegant graphical debugger, this is the only feature that is really unique to IDEs. And you pay for this elegance with a huge memory and disk space footprint Software like Eclipse can be as bloated as Microsoft Office. Is it worth using up half a gigabyte of RAM just to get a graphical debugger? If you use your debugger all day, every day, the answer might be "yes." If you only use a debugger occasionally, you're probably better off not bothering with all the bloatware.

If you have the Git Bash shell plus your favorite editor, that may be all you need to do most of your development work. The shell takes up only about a megabyte of RAM. That's a *mega*byte, not a *giga*byte. If you use an editor like Vim or gVim (its slightly larger GUI version), your files will take up about 2 megabytes of RAM plus the size of your source code. Again, that is megabytes, not gigabytes. With tools like this, you can work very efficiently even on a system with limited RAM. On my old Windows XP system (which had only 1 GB of RAM), I could have a couple of Git Bash shell windows open and 20 open gVim windows, and the system would barely bat an eyelash. Firefox hogged the largest share of the memory on that machine (up to 400 MB). If you tried to run Eclipse as well, there probably wouldn't have been room to run anything else, especially if you fantasized about having a Microsoft Office or LibreOffice document open as well. While newer systems have considerably more RAM, you shouldn't waste it if you don't have to. Much like Parkinson's Law, software has a tendency to suck up all available memory, no matter how good your hardware is.

How to Download and Install msysgit for Windows

Downloading and installing Git (also referred to as 'msysgit') and all its components, is very easy, since a Windows Setup file is available. First, go to the official Web site for Git:

http://git-scm.com/

In the lower right part of your browser window, you'll see what looks like a flat screen TV announcing the latest version of Git, with a "Download for Windows" button. Click on the button to save the installation file to your local machine. Note that the Web site tries to auto-detect what kind of machine is making the request, so if you are downloading the installation file from a different operating system than the one on which you want to use Git, you'll need to use the red "Downloads" button on the left instead.

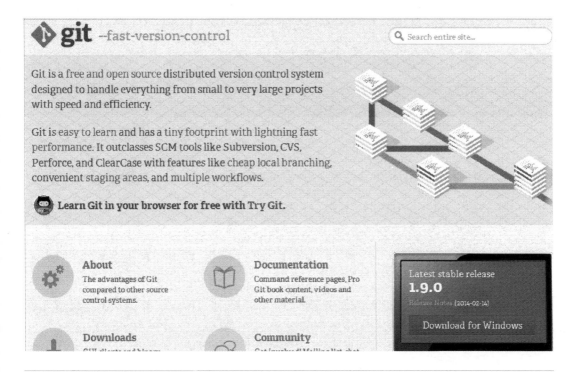

When you click the button to download, you'll see a dialog asking you where to save the file.

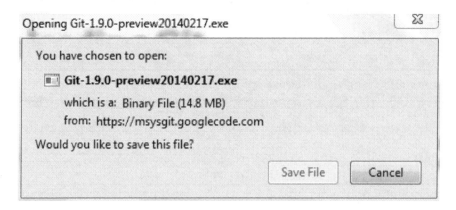

Note that the file name says that it is a "preview." Don't be concerned by this. Git has been thoroughly tested and has been quite stable for years. While there are certainly periodic bug fixes and minor changes to how some features work, Git is used daily by thousands if not millions of developers, so you can have a pretty high degree of confidence that it will work as advertised. As with most software, you will likely only encounter problems if you are trying to use very obscure features.

You'll see the common security warning that the software is from an 'unknown' publisher:

After clicking 'Run' to start the installer, you encounter the Setup wizard:

Click 'Next' to get to the license agreement:

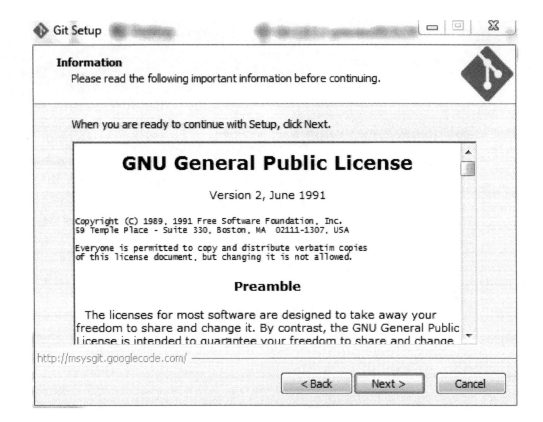

After clicking 'Next,' you'll see the 'Select Components' window:

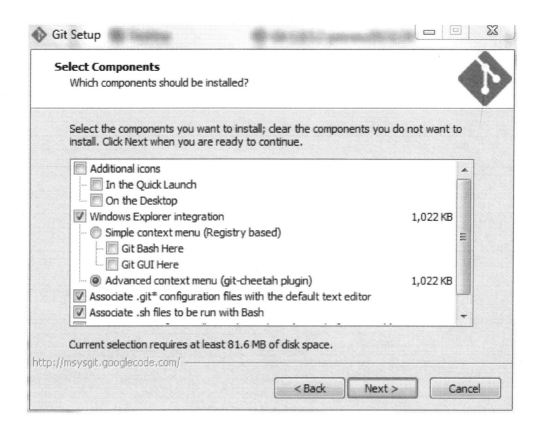

This gives you a chance to choose which pieces of the software you wish to install. I recommend accepting all the default values. If you want to be able use Git from the Windows Explorer menu, you may want to consider clicking in the 'Git Bash Here' and 'Git GUI Here' check boxes.

After making your component selection and clicking 'Next,' you'll arrive at the 'Adjusting your PATH environment window:

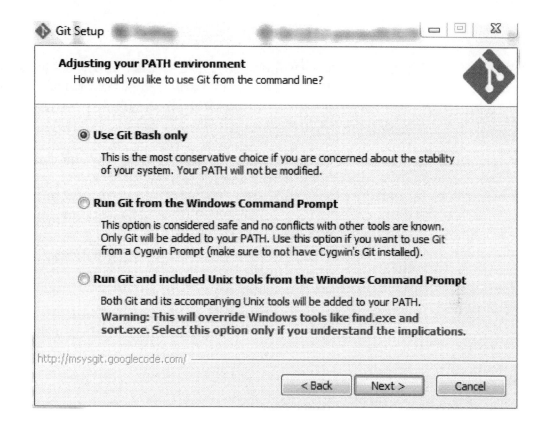

This is actually one of the most important parts of the installation. It determines how you will be able to access both the Git application itself and the utilities included with it. I strongly recommend sticking with the default conservative value and choosing 'Use Git Bash only.' This means that you will use Git and its accessory programs *only* from the Git Bash shell (and possibly from the Windows Explorer menu, if you selected that option). You will *not* have access to Git from a Windows DOS box, otherwise known as cmd.exe. While this choice might make some Windows users nervous, once you get some experience using the Bash shell, you will probably never want to go back to cmd.exe again.

Note, however, that you will have to adjust the PATH variable used in the Bash shell (which is separate from the Windows PATH variable) in order to use other programs – such as your favorite editor – from Bash. This is not that hard to do, and I'll show you how later in the book.

If you are running the Linux-like environment provided by Cygwin, or if you have a strong need to use Git from cmd.exe, you can select the second choice, 'Run Git from the Windows Command Prompt.'

I recommend avoiding the third choice entirely, since it can cause conflicts between some of the standard Windows utilities and the utilities provided by Git. Windows utilities like find.exe and sort.exe are attempts to emulate UNIX utilities anyway, so why not use the real utilities provided by Git?

Once you have chosen an option, click 'Next' and you'll arrive at the *other* important part of the installation, 'Configuring the line ending conversions.'

Why do you have to worry about line endings? Git runs on multiple platforms, including Linux, Windows, and Mac OS X. Files can be changed on one platform and committed to a repository on a different platform. The problem is that all three platforms have had different conventions for how lines in a text file should end. You would think this ought to be a trivial issue, but because of the historical baggage of how each of these operating systems was developed, it isn't.

The dominant operating systems today use up to two ASCII characters to represent line endings. One of them is the linefeed, commonly represented as '<LF>.' It is also referred to as a newline character or '\n' in the parlance of the C programming language (a very widely adopted convention in other programming languages as well). The other one is the carriage return, commonly represented as '<CR>' in documentation, and known as '\r' in the C language. When you use any text processing application on your computer and hit the '<Enter>' key on your keyboard, the characters used by your operating system to denote end-of-line will be added to the text.

UNIX and Linux use the linefeed or newline character ('\n') to denote end-of-line, and current versions of the Mac OS X system use this convention as well.

Older versions of the Macintosh OS used the carriage return ('\r') to denote end-of-line instead of a linefeed. You won't have to worry about this unless you are using a very old machine.

In contrast, Microsoft Windows and DOS (along with OS/2, the original CP/M, and even Palm OS) all use a carriage return/linefeed combination ('<CR><LF>' or '\r\n' depending on your notational preference) to represent end-of-line.

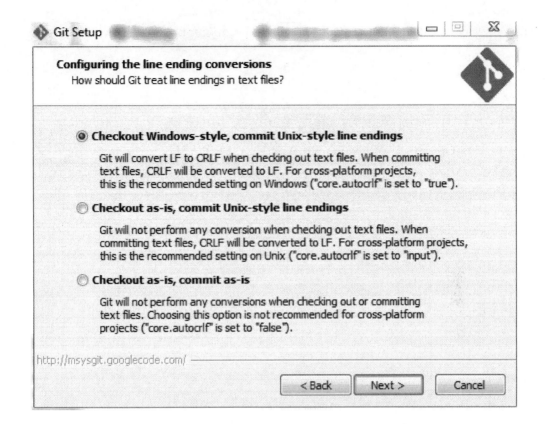

Trying to use files on one operating system that were created on a different operating system with a different end-of-line convention can lead to problems. When you open such a file in your favorite text editor, you may see spurious extra characters at the end of each line or other weirdness.

The point of this discussion is that Git is smart enough to protect you from having to deal with these problems. If you accept the default choice of 'Checkout Windows-style, commit Unix-style line endings,' everything should just work and you won't have to worry about it. Your source code will be stored in a standard format, no matter where the repository is located, and will be converted to the conventions of your local system whenever you check out the code. I strongly recommend *not* choosing any of the other options unless you have a specific reason to do so.

Of course, this whole discussion is moot if you aren't interested in using Git at all and only want to use the Git Bash shell. In that case, your choice won't have any effect on your work. But it is better to accept the default choice, just in case you change your mind and decide to use Git after all.

After clicking 'Next' to continue the installation, you might see an unusual warning from Git:

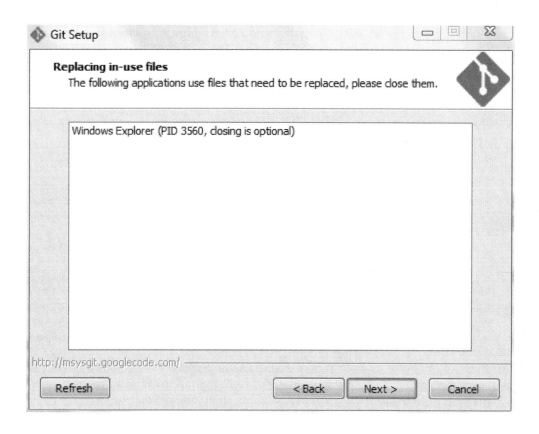

Don't panic and just close whatever application Git asks you to close (if you can close it). I haven't normally seen this dialog during previous installations of Git (it might conceivably be a bug in the latest release), but it doesn't seem to cause any harm. Click 'Next' and you'll finally reach the end of the Git installation process.

If you leave the check box checked when you click on the 'Finish" button, the release notes for the version of Git that you just installed will be displayed. Note that the Git release notes are stored as a Rich Text Document, so allowing display of the release notes will invoke your copy of Microsoft Word, LibreOffice, or whatever other application is used as the default on your system for opening .rtf files. It is always a good idea to at least skim over the release notes for a newly installed product, so that you have an idea of what major changes have occurred, if any.

Now that you have successfully installed Git, you should see a Git Bash icon on your desktop. Double-click on it, and a Bash command window will open. Much of the rest of the book will be devoted to explaining how you can use this window to run commands without need of a graphical user interface.

How to Download and Install msysgit for Windows

Configuring the Git Bash Shortcut

If you right-click on the Git Bash icon and select the 'Properties' menu item, you'll see a standard Windows property dialog. This will allow you to change many characteristics of your Bash command window, including the font and text size, screen width and height, and even the colors used.

I suggest accepting the defaults, at least until you get some experience with using the Bash shell. In particular, I use the default 80-character wide by 25-line window display, since code has been written to fit in such a display since time immemorial. Obviously you don't have to do this if you have a large monitor, but on a laptop with limited screen real estate, I find it convenient to follow this tradition. Note that like any window on the Windows system, your Bash command window can be maximized to vertically fill the whole screen. (However, the width of the window won't increase beyond that of your chosen setting.)

Copying and Pasting to/from the Git Bash Shell Window

One issue that you may wish to change right away is how text is copied and pasted to and from Bash command windows. The Bash command window relies on the same underlying software used by the Windows cmd.exe windows, and thus uses the same conventions for copy and paste operations.

If you want to copy some text from your Bash command window into another application, you'll have to start by selecting it with your mouse or trackpad. After the text is selected, click on the icon in the upper left corner of the window. From the resulting dropdown menu, choose 'Edit->Copy.' The text will be stored in the Windows Clipboard. Then click in the window for the application for where you want to paste the text, and press <Ctrl-v> to paste, where <Ctrl-v> means to hold down the <Ctrl> key and press the 'v' key. (Note that using <Ctrl-v> to paste doesn't work in every application – including the Bash command window itself!)

In order to paste text from the Windows Clipboard into a Bash command window, click on the icon in the upper left corner of the window to get the dropdown menu, and choose 'Edit->Paste' to paste the text.

Both of these operations can be very tedious and annoying, so let's change this behavior to be a little more convenient. Once again right-click on the Git Bash icon and choose the 'Properties' menu. When the 'Git Bash Properties' dialog appears, click on the 'Options' tab. On the right-hand side of the tab, you'll see two check boxes under the 'Edit Options' section. Check both boxes, for 'QuickEdit mode' and 'Insert mode,' and then click 'OK' at the bottom of the dialog.

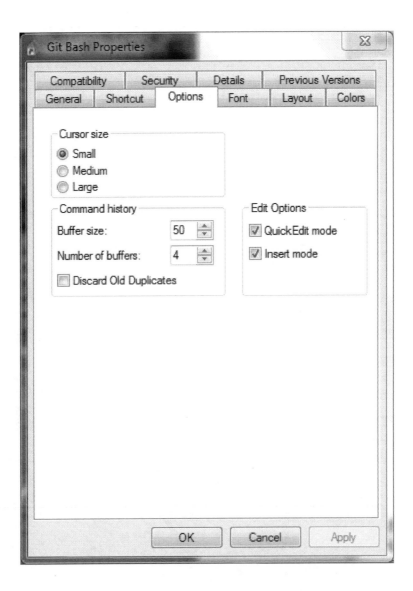

Now when you select text for copying in the Bash command window, you can simply press the <Enter> key to copy it to the Windows Clipboard, and then paste as usual into other applications.

When you wish to paste from the Windows Clipboard into a Bash command window, you can allegedly click in your Bash command window and hit the <Insert> key (labelled 'Ins' on my laptop) to paste the text. On some systems, <Ctrl-Insert> might work instead. I find that neither keystroke works on my Toshiba laptop, so I am sadly confined to using the 'Edit->Paste' menu choice rather than using a more efficient keyboard command. So the Git Bash shell doesn't quite take away all the pain of working on a Windows system.

Alternate Consoles for Git Bash

There are a variety of alternate consoles available for Windows. These are essentially replacements for cmd.exe that provide additional features, but from which you can still run the Git Bash shell. Two of the more popular alternate consoles appear to be Console, available here

```
http://sourceforge.net/projects/console/
```

and ConEmu. available here:

```
http://code.google.com/p/conemu-maximus5/
```

I have never used these products, so I can't offer any real opinion about how good they are, but those who are sick of cmd.exe should at least be aware that other choices are available.

Basic Bash

BASH is actually an acronym for the 'Bourne-Again Shell' (even though 'Bash' is usually not written with all uppercase letters). This is a pun on the original UNIX Bourne shell, which was written by Stephen Bourne of Bell Labs back in 1977. It was the default shell for UNIX Version 7.

Bash is the default shell for most modern Linux systems, the Cygwin environment, and Mac OS X. But the original Bourne shell is still available on many systems for those who want it. It is important to note that many shells have been developed for UNIX-like systems, including the C shell, the Korn shell and the Z shell. Bash uses the programming features of the Bourne shell, and some of the popular interactive features of the C shell and Korn shell.

Bash is effectively a superset of the Bourne shell. Shell commands can be saved in script files and run as programs in their own right. Virtually all Bourne shell scripts can be run by the Bash shell. Similarly, Bash scripts can often be run in the Bourne shell, as long as they don't use commands that are unique to Bash.

The primary function of any shell is to act as a command-line interpreter. The shell prompts the user for input and waits for commands to be typed in. It then executes the command(s) and displays the output on the screen (or sends it somewhere else).

Why would you want to use a shell that is based on technology that is over 30 years old and in fact predates the existence of PCs entirely? Because it provides far more power than PC shells had until the mid-90's. DOS never even came close to rivaling the capabilities of even the original Bourne shell, let alone the much-improved Bash. Only Windows PowerShell (written a couple of decades after the Bourne shell) manages to mimic the power and flexibility of UNIX shells, and it suffers from the constraint of only being available on Windows. Bash can run on every popular operating system.

If you already have some experience at using Bash, you can skip most of this chapter and dive right in. However, be sure to read the first couple of notes about Windows drive names and file names with spaces, so that you'll understand how to refer to files and directories under Windows.

Note that because Bash provides so much power and flexibility, I am not going to

---

attempt to cover more than a small fraction of the shell's capabilities. We'll focus on the most basic features that you need to get up and running. Entire books have been written on Bash alone, and I'll refer you to those references for those who want more advanced details.

A Note on Directories and How Git Bash Handles Windows Drive Names

Windows refers to hard drive partitions with letters of the alphabet. 'C:\' typically refers to your primary hard disk. On my system, the main drive is divided into two partitions, the C: drive (where applications reside) and the E: drive (where my data resides). The first thing you need to know about the Git Bash shell is that it uses different nomenclature to refer to Windows drive partitions and path names. To refer to the top directory of the C: drive, you must use the syntax

```
/c
```

That is, a forward slash followed by a lowercase letter 'c.' Windows path names are of the form

```
Drive_Letter:\Directory_Name
```

(Note the colon and the backslash.) Git Bash path names are of the form

```
/drive_letter/directory_name
```

Bash path names don't use colons at all, and always use forward slashes rather than backslashes.

How to Handle File and Path Names with Spaces

Consider a typical Windows directory like

```
C:\Program Files
```

How would you refer to this directory in Bash? The proper syntax is

```
"/c/Program Files"
```

Once again, drive letters like 'C:' are replaced by '/c,' and backslash characters are replaced by forward slashes. However, if you want to refer to a file or directory that includes spaces in its name, you must enclose that name in quotation marks! Technically, only the 'Program Files' directory name needs to be quoted, so you could use syntax like

```
/c/"Program Files"
```

instead. However, it is better to get into the habit of quoting the entire path to avoid mistakes. This will make it easy to add names-with-spaces to the path without having to change your quotes.

Built-in Commands

The Bash shell contains a number of built-in commands that are executed by the shell itself. All other commands (known as external commands) are run by starting a subprocess. This means that built-in commands have slightly faster performance. Let's take a quick look at a few of Bash's builtins. (I won't use a hyphen when referring to builtins as nouns.) We'll start by checking where we are with the command

```
$ pwd
```

which is short for 'print working directory.' The output of this command shows your current location in the file system. This command is arguably not necessary in the Git Bash shell, since the user and current directory is listed above every prompt anyway. But on other platforms this information will likely not be present, and you'll need to use 'pwd' instead. (One alternative is that you can alter the Bash prompt to display the current directory if you like. The Git Bash shell on Windows uses a two-line prompt which displays the user, hostname, and directory on the first line, and the traditional Bash prompt on the second line. More on this later.)

Another command commonly used in conjunction with 'pwd' is 'cd,' which is short for 'change directory.' On the surface, this command looks identical to the 'CD' command in Windows, but it has a couple of convenient tricks up its sleeve. Let's first look at the 'Program Files' directory with the command

```
$ cd "/c/Program Files"
```

(Remember, don't type the dollar sign that indicates the Bash prompt. Also remember that we enclose the path in quotation marks when it contains spaces.) You can confirm you are really there by typing

```
$ pwd
/c/Program Files
```

The response from Bash (the second line without a prompt in front of it) shows that we are where we expected to be. This directory is used for all modern Windows applications. However, let's also take a peek at the directory for applications that run in x86 compatibility mode (programs that were designed for older versions of Windows):

```
$ cd "/c/Program Files (x86)"
```

Now suppose you would like to go back to the last directory you were in. Simply type

```
$ cd -
/c/Program Files
```

Bash responds with the new directory location, confirming that we're back where we started. Since both of these directories are at the same level of the directory hierarchy, we could have returned to the same location by using the command

```
$ cd "../Program Files"
```

instead. The two periods are Bash's shorthand notation for referring to the parent directory of where you currently are. So this command effectively means "go up to the /c directory and then down to the 'Program Files' directory. It is good to be familiar with this notation, but it requires more typing than 'cd -.' I should also note that 'cd -' works no matter what your previous directory was. Suppose that you started by typing

```
$ cd "/c/Program Files (x86)"
```

and then

```
$ cd /c/vegetable/rutabaga
```

(assuming you have directories named 'vegetable' and 'rutabaga'). Then 'cd -' will still return you to the x86 directory. Note that the command to change to the 'rutabaga' directory did not require any quote marks, since there were no spaces in the path.

When you first start up a Bash shell window, the directory that you are in is called your **home directory.** To get back to this directory from anywhere else, simply type

```
$ cd
```

On my system, my home directory looks like

```
$ pwd
/e/Users/Michael Hanna
```

since my user accounts are on the E: drive in Windows. Bash has a useful shorthand that comes in handy when using the cd command: the tilde or squiggle key ('~'), which is usually to the left of the '1' key on U.S. keyboards. The tilde character is a shorthand for your home directory, so you don't have to type out a long directory path every time. You may find it useful if you want to switch directly from some other directory to a *subdirectory* of your home directory. For example, from any other location, I could type

```
$ cd ~/vegetable/rutabaga
```

It is easy to verify where I really am:

```
$ pwd
/e/Users/Michael Hanna/vegetable/rutabaga
```

(Yes, I really created these silly directories for this example!)

Let's also briefly discuss a Bash built-in command that even many experienced Bash users don't know about. This is the 'type' command. It has nothing to do with the old DOS 'TYPE' command the prints a file to the screen. Rather, it describes what Bash knows about a command name. If you use the '-a' option, this builtin will tell you whether a command is a Bash builtin or an external command. You can even run the command on itself!

```
$ type -a type
type is a shell builtin
```

If we look at 'pwd,' we see that there are actually *two* versions of this command present:

```
$ type -a pwd
pwd is a shell builtin
pwd is /bin/pwd
```

The GNU utilities provided by Git Bash include an implementation of the 'pwd' command, but this command is also built into the shell itself. The version of 'pwd' included with Git is just a shell script that calls the Bash built-in function with all the arguments that the user provided. I don't know why the Git people considered this to be necessary.

An example of an external command is the 'ls' utility, which is used to list files in a directory (in much the same fashion as the DOS 'DIR' command):

```
$ type -a ls
ls is /bin/ls
```

I have to confess that I got this wrong when I was first writing this section of the book. The 'ls' command is so commonly used that I assumed that it was a shell builtin, but it isn't.

Another common built-in command is 'echo,' which prints a string. For example,

```
$ echo "My hovercraft is full of eels."
My hovercraft is full of eels.
```

The echo command is commonly used in shell scripts to produce output for the user when the script executes. We'll discover other built-in commands as we continue our discussion of Bash's features.

Directory Handling Commands

Since we have already had a little practice at moving around directories and looking at their contents, you will be pleased to know that Bash has several built-in functions to help you with managing directories. These functions are borrowed from the C shell. The basic concept is that you can have a **directory stack**. A stack is a last-in, first-out data structure, much like a stack of dishes at your local cafeteria or salad bar. The last item that you pushed on top of the stack will become the first item that you remove or pop. The 'dirs' command will show you the current contents of the directory stack. By default, there is only one item in the stack; namely, your current directory. For example, suppose that you are currently in the '/bin' directory. The 'dirs' command will produce the result

```
$ dirs
/bin
```

Not too inspiring. Now let's use the 'pushd' builtin to push a new directory onto the stack.

```
$ pushd "/c/Program Files"
/c/Program Files /bin
```

"/c/Program Files" is now the current directory, which you can confirm with the 'pwd' command. The output of pushd shows you the current directory stack, with the latest directory added at the leftmost end of the list. You can easily confirm that the 'dirs' command shows the same stack:

```
$ dirs
/c/Program Files /bin
```

What if you want to temporarily go back to the /bin directory before you finish your work in the current directory? In this case, you can just give a numeric argument to pushd;

```
$ pushd +1
/bin /c/Program Files
```

'pushd +n' *rotates* the directory stack so that the nth element from the left is at the top, which in this case makes /bin your current directory. (You can also use a negative number to rotate the stack the other way.) You can do another 'pushd +1' to get back to the other directory. After doing this, perhaps you'd like to add a third directory to the list. You could do this with a command like

```
$ pushd "/c/Program Files (x86)"
/c/Program Files (x86) /c/Program Files /bin
```

You now have three directories in the stack. You can see a little more elegant list of the stack elements by using the 'dirs -v' command:

```
$ dirs -v
 0  /c/Program Files (x86)
 1  /c/Program Files
 2  /bin
```

In this format, the most recently added directory really is at the top of the stack. Once you are done with your work in the current directory, you can use the 'popd' command to pop it off the stack:

```
$ popd
/c/Program Files /bin
```

Now suppose you wish to back to your home directory before you continue work in the other two directories in your stack. Instead of typing out the full path to your home directory, Bash's tilde shortcut comes to the rescue again

```
$ pushd ~
~ /c/Program Files /bin
```

If you need to deal with a lot of directories, these commands can save you some headaches. Note that each Git Bash window has its own directory stack, so you can easily use multiple Bash windows to deal with related groups of directories.

Command Line Completion

When you type a command at the Bash prompt, you can simply hit the <Tab> key to complete a partial command name or file name that you have started to type. For example, if you type the following from your home directory,

```
$ ls .ba
```

hitting the <Tab> key will produce

```
$ ls .bash
```

if a .bashrc file is present. If you know that there are multiple files present beginning with '.bash,' you can hit the <Tab> key again to a list of all the possible completions of the file name:

```
$ ls .bash
.bash_history                    .bashrc_backup_2014-02-17
.bashrc                          .bashrc_book_example
```

At this point, you can either type out the rest of the file name by hand, or you can type just enough of the name to make it unique and then hit <Tab> to complete the name. For example, you could add two letters to match the start of '.bash_history:'

```
$ ls .bash_h
```

If you hit the <Tab> again now, Bash will complete the command for you:

```
$ ls .bash_history
```

Note that once the command is completed to your satisfaction, you still have to hit the <Enter> key to actually *execute* that command.

Bash also has a much fancier programmable completion facility for those who are obsessed with having every possible way to complete a command line. We won't cover this, since in my opinion it is overkill for beginners. (I'm not a beginner, and I have never felt a need for this feature.)

Bash Command History

Bash has a very nice history mechanism that can save you a lot of typing. Want to rerun a previous command? Simply use the up and down arrow keys to find the command you are interested in, and hit <Enter> when you see it. Or, if you would like to change the command, backspace over part of it, type out the new part, and hit <Enter>.

Bash also supports the GNU readline library. What this means is that you can also edit current or previous Bash commands by doing more than just backspacing over them. By default, the readline library supports editing with a subset of commands from the emacs editor. You can get a nice cheat sheet summarizing the available emacs editing commands here:

```
http://www.catonmat.net/download/readline-emacs-editing-mode-cheat-sheet.pdf
```

If you prefer the vi editor, readline will also let you use vi commands if you put the following line into your .bashrc file:

```
set -o vi          #  Do line editing in vi mode
```

(See the section on "Configuring Bash with the .bashrc File" for more details on how to configure Bash to your personal preferences.) If you decide to edit Bash commands using the vi editor, you can also get a nice cheat sheet for the available vi commands:

```
http://www.catonmat.net/download/bash-vi-editing-mode-cheat-sheet.pdf
```

Note that if you use the vi editing capabilities, by default you are in text insertion mode, which is not vi's normal default. To move to different parts of the command line, you'll first need to hit the <Esc> key (in the upper left corner of your keyboard) to put vi into command mode. Then you can move the cursor using vi commands (for example, type '4b' to move backward four words). When you are done making changes, hit the <Enter> key and the current version of your command line will be executed. If you flub up, don't worry. Just hit the <Up Arrow> key to recall the previous command and try again.

You can use the built-in 'history' command to display a list of all previous commands, each preceded by a number. You might get output like

```
107    dirs
108    pwd
109    pushd +1
110    pwd
111    pushd +1
112    pushd "/c/Program Files x86"
113    pushd "/c/Program Files (x86)"
114    dirs -v
115    popd
```

The list of previous commands is stored in ~/.bash_history by default.

There are a wide variety of ways to refer to previous commands, and we will list only a few of the more common ones. To repeat a command, just type '!!' (pronounced "bang bang") after typing the command the first time:

```
$ ls -ld Microsoft*
drwxr-xr-x   11 Michael   Administ       4096 Jul 14  2009 Microsoft Games
drwxr-xr-x    5 Michael   Administ       4096 Feb 12 12:44 Microsoft
Silverlight

$ !!
ls -ld Microsoft*
drwxr-xr-x   11 Michael   Administ       4096 Jul 14  2009 Microsoft Games
drwxr-xr-x    5 Michael   Administ       4096 Feb 12 12:44 Microsoft
Silverlight
```

You can execute the second previous command by using '!-2' to refer to the command:

```
$ cd "$PROGRAM_FILES"

$ ls *.txt
ls: *.txt: No such file or directory

$ cd ..

$ !-2
ls *.txt
eula.1028.txt   eula.1033.txt   eula.1040.txt
eula.1042.txt   eula.3082.txt
eula.1031.txt   eula.1036.txt   eula.1041.txt
eula.2052.txt
```

This allows you to easily alternate between two commands. If you had a deeper directory structure, you could keep moving back up one level and doing the 'ls' command again just by repeated use of '!-2.'

You can choose a previous command directly from the history list by typing '! command_number:'

```
$ !114
dirs -v
 0  /c
 1  /c/Program Files
 2  /bin
```

You can pick the last command *starting with* a given string via '!command_string:'

```
$ !ls
ls *.txt
eula.1028.txt   eula.1033.txt   eula.1040.txt
eula.1042.txt   eula.3082.txt
eula.1031.txt   eula.1036.txt   eula.1041.txt
eula.2052.txt
```

You can pick the last command that *contains* a given string by using the syntax '!?command_string?:'

```
$ !?Program Files?
pushd "/c/Program Files (x86)"
/c/Program Files (x86) /c/Program Files /c/Program Files /bin
```

Best of all, you can easily fix a mistake in your previous command by substituting a new value for the old one with the '^old_string^new_string^ syntax:

```
$ cd "/c/Progrm Files"
sh.exe": cd: /c/Progrm Files: No such file or directory

$ ^Progrm^Program^
cd "/c/Program Files"
```

Note that only the first occurrence of the search string is replaced. There is also a more general substitution command that can be applied to any element of the history list by adding ':s/old/new/' after any history command. For example,

```
$ cd /bin
$ ls ms*
msmtp.exe               msys-minires.dll   msys-ssl-
0.9.8.dll
msys-1.0.dll            msys-perl5_8.dll   msys-z.dll
```

```
msys-crypto-0.9.8.dll  msys-regex-1.dll  msysltdl-3.dll

$ pwd
/bin

$ !-2:s/ms/msys/
ls msys*
msys-1.0.dll            msys-minires.dll  msys-regex-1.dll   msys-z.dll
msys-crypto-0.9.8.dll   msys-perl5_8.dll  msys-ssl-0.9.8.dll msysltdl-3.dll
```

The second ls command only shows the files beginning with 'msys' and ignores msmtp.exe. This type of substitution again changes only the first occurrence of the string, but you can change *all* occurrences if you use the syntax ':gs/old/new/' as shown below:

```
$ ls msys-zzl*
ls: msys-zzl*: No such file or directory
$ !!:gs/z/s/
ls msys-ssl*
msys-ssl-0.9.8.dll
```

The table below summarizes what we have learned:

History Substitution Commands	
!!	Execute previous command
!-n	Execute the nth previous command
!n	Execute command number n from the history list
!string	Execute last command starting with 'string'
!?string?	Execute last command *containing* 'string'
^old_value^new_value^	Replace first occurrence of 'old_value' with 'new_value' in previous command
!history:s/old/new/	Replace first occurrence of 'old' with 'new' in referenced command (such as '!!' or '!-2')
!history:gs/old/new/	Replace all occurrences of 'old' with 'new' in referenced command (such as '!!' or '!-2')

Job Control with Foreground and Background Jobs

Although the original UNIX shells were developed long before the advent of graphical user interfaces, they supported multiprocessing by allowing you to run multiple tasks simultaneously. This was a very important capability at the time, since you couldn't have multiple windows open to perform different tasks. Instead, all tasks had to be done from a single command line. The **foreground job** is the command that is currently running. **Background jobs** are other tasks that are no longer being controlled by the command line. You can **suspend** the foreground job and start a new shell by typing <Ctrl-z>; that is, by holding down the Control key and hitting the 'z' key. This is something that is usually done when you are editing a file. If you open a file, say with the Vim editor, and then type <Ctrl-z>, you will see a new shell prompt:

```
$ vim .bash_history
new shell started

Welcome to Git (version 1.9.0-preview20140217)


Run 'git help git' to display the help index.
Run 'git help <command>' to display help for specific
commands.
```

Do whatever other tasks you need to do and then type 'exit' to leave the shell. You will return to your editing session (which you can end by typing ':wq' to save changes and quit). This makes it easy to temporarily interrupt your work and do something else.

You can also explicitly move jobs into the foreground or background. To put a job into the background, simply add an ampersand ('&') after the end of the command. For example, if you run gVim (the GUI version of the Vim editor) in the foreground, you can't type any more commands into your Bash window until you exit the editor:

```
$ gvim new_file.txt
```

Put the command into the background and you can immediately enter new commands into your Bash window:

```
$ !! &
gvim new_file.txt &
```

```
[1] 5712
```

Here we cheated a bit and used the '!!' history command to re-execute the previous command by adding an ampersand to the end. This saved us from having to retype the entire command. Notice that when you put the command in the background, you see a number enclosed in brackets followed by a process ID. The number in brackets is the job number. You can see all the jobs currently running in the background by typing

```
$ jobs
[1]+  Running                 gvim new_file.txt &
```

If you edit a second file before finishing with the first file, you will have two jobs running in the background:

```
$ gvim second_file.txt &
[2] 6628

$ jobs
[1]-  Running                 gvim new_file.txt &
[2]+  Running                 gvim second_file.txt &
```

You can move a background job to the foreground by typing 'fg %job_number' at the Bash prompt (don't forget to put the percent sign in front of the job number):

```
$ fg %2
gvim second_file.txt
```

Because gVim is now the foreground process, you can't enter any more commands into your Bash window until you click on the gVim window and type ':wq' to save your work and quit the editor. If you exit from your original gVim window while it was running in the background, then next time you enter a command in your Bash window (or the next time you hit the <Enter> key), you will see a message notifying you that the background job has completed.

```
$

[1]+  Done                    gvim new_file.txt
```

(There is also a 'bg' shell builtin to explicitly put commands into the background, but you should rarely need this.)

You can explicitly stop a job with the 'kill %job_number' command. Be aware that this will wipe out your file if you destroy an editing session:

```
$ gvim new_file.txt &
[1] 4224

$ jobs
[1]+  Running                 gvim new_file.txt &

$ kill %1
[1]+  Terminated              gvim new_file.txt

$ ls -l new_file.txt
ls: new_file.txt: No such file or directory
```

(One nice feature of Vim is that it saves a copy of your text in a so-called 'swap file' even when you don't explicitly save the file. In this case, the file would be named '.new_file.txt.swp' - note the period at the front of the file name, which means that Bash considers it a hidden file. If you try to edit new_file.txt again, Vim will detect the swap file and ask you if you want to use its contents.)

If you need to run a complex software build (perhaps with a make file), just add an ampersand to your command to run it in the background. Then you can do other tasks while you wait for the job to complete, and Bash will notify you when it is done. We can summarize the job control commands in a convenient table:

Job Control Commands	
<Ctrl-z>	Suspend current task and open a new shell
command &	Run command as a background task
jobs	List jobs running in the background
fg %job_number	Make job the current foreground task
bg %job_number	Make current foreground task into a background job
kill %job_number	Stop the job, possibly destroying data

Other Shell Builtins

There are many other useful commands built into Bash, and we'll cover some of them later in the book. If you want to see a complete list of functions built into Bash, simply type 'help' at the prompt:

```
$ help
GNU bash, version 3.1.0(1)-release (i686-pc-msys)
These shell commands are defined internally. Type `help' to see this list.
Type `help name' to find out more about the function `name'.
Use `info bash' to find out more about the shell in general.
Use `man -k' or `info' to find out more about commands not in this list.

A star (*) next to a name means that the command is disabled.

 JOB_SPEC [&]                           (( expression ))
 . filename [arguments]                 :
 [ arg... ]                             [[ expression ]]
 alias [-p] [name[=value] ... ]         bg [job_spec ...]
 bind [-lpvsPVS] [-m keymap] [-f fi     break [n]
 builtin [shell-builtin [arg ...]]      caller [EXPR]
 case WORD in [PATTERN [| PATTERN].     cd [-L|-P] [dir]
 command [-pVv] command [arg ...]       compgen [-abcdefgjksuv] [-o option
 complete [-abcdefgjksuv] [-pr] [-o     continue [n]
 declare [-afFirtx] [-p] [name[=val     dirs [-clpv] [+N] [-N]
 disown [-h] [-ar] [jobspec ...]        echo [-neE] [arg ...]
 enable [-pnds] [-a] [-f filename]      eval [arg ...]
 exec [-cl] [-a name] file [redirec     exit [n]
 export [-nf] [name[=value] ...] or     false
 fc [-e ename] [-nlr] [first] [last     fg [job_spec]
 for NAME [in WORDS ... ;] do COMMA     for (( exp1; exp2; exp3 )); do COM
 function NAME { COMMANDS ; } or NA     getopts optstring name [arg]
 hash [-lr] [-p pathname] [-dt] [na     help [-s] [pattern ...]
 history [-c] [-d offset] [n] or hi     if COMMANDS; then COMMANDS; [ elif
 jobs [-lnprs] [jobspec ...] or job     kill [-s sigspec | -n signum | -si
 let arg [arg ...]                      local name[=value] ...
 logout                                 popd [+N | -N] [-n]
 printf [-v var] format [arguments]     pushd [dir | +N | -N] [-n]
 pwd [-LPW]                             read [-ers] [-u fd] [-t timeout] [
 readonly [-af] [name[=value] ...]      return [n]
 select NAME [in WORDS ... ;] do CO     set [--abefhkmnptuvxBCHP] [-o opti
 shift [n]                              shopt [-pqsu] [-o long-option] opt
 source filename [arguments]            suspend [-f]
 test [expr]                            time [-p] PIPELINE
 times                                  trap [-lp] [arg signal_spec ...]
 true                                   type [-afptP] name [name ...]
 typeset [-afFirtx] [-p] name[=valu     ulimit [-SHacdfilmnpqstuvx] [limit
 umask [-p] [-S] [mode]                 unalias [-a] name [name ...]
 unset [-f] [-v] [name ...]             until COMMANDS; do COMMANDS; done
 variables - Some variable names an     wait [n]
```

```
while COMMANDS; do COMMANDS; done   { COMMANDS ; }
```

External Commands

External commands are not part of the shell itself, so they must be run in a subprocess. This makes such commands run slightly more slowly, but from the user's perspective there is no other major difference.

Let's start by considering how to create directories, since we were just examining directories in the previous section. If I want to create a path like 'vegetable/rutabaga' in my home directory, I have to create *two* separate directories. Directories are created with the 'mkdir' command (short for 'make directory'). If you try to create two directories with one command, you will get an error like

```
$ mkdir vegetable/rutabaga
mkdir: cannot create directory `vegetable/rutabaga': No
such file or directory
```

Instead, create the directories in sequence:

```
$ mkdir vegetable
```

```
$ cd vegetable
```

```
$ mkdir rutabaga
```

Create the first one and cd to it. After you are in the new directory, *then* you can create the second one. Note that you won't actually be in the new 'rutabaga' directory until you cd into it:

```
$ cd rutabaga
```

Now let's consider how to list the contents of a directory. In a Windows DOS box, we would use the 'DIR' command to list the contents of a directory. The equivalent command in Bash is

```
$ ls
```

(short for 'list'). Like 'DIR,' this command lists the contents of the current directory, or some other directory that you specify.

Arguments to Commands

At first glance, the 'ls' command shown a moment ago seems more limited than its Windows counterpart, because it only lists the file name itself, and no other information like the size of the file or when it was created. However, the ls command has many hidden talents. Like most UNIX-style commands, it accepts many optional arguments. To get output similar to the Windows 'DIR' command, ask for a long listing by typing

```
$ ls -l
```

We won't worry about what all the output means for now, but note that you are now getting *more* information than what the 'DIR' command provides.

If all you want is a one-column list of file names (suitable for sending to other programs, use

```
$ ls -1
```

Note that the above argument is a 'one,' not an 'el.' Another useful option produces a list of files that has '/' appended after each directory name, and '*' appended after each executable file:

```
$ ls -F
```

You can also highlight different types of files by color if you use

```
$ ls --color
```

Hidden Files

You may recall that Windows has a concept of hidden files that are not visible to the user by default. This concept is also derived from UNIX. In UNIX and Linux systems, hidden files (and directory names) must start with a period. (They can still have a DOS-style extension like '.txt' if you wish.) The Bash shell follows this same

---

Basic Bash   **47**

convention. How can you see these hidden files? Just use

```
$ ls -a
```

This will list all files, including hidden files and directories.

More About Command Arguments

We have seen that there are actually two types of arguments to UNIX-style commands: The so-called **short arguments,** which begin with one hyphen and are followed by a single letter of the alphabet. The other type is the newer style of **long argument,** which starts with two hyphens and is followed by an English word or phrase. (Argument phrases usually have words separated with hyphens.) These two types of arguments can be mixed and matched, but you have to exercise a little bit of care.

Single-letter options can be combined into one argument: A single hyphen followed by multiple letters. For example,

```
$ ls -al
```

gives a long listing of all files including hidden files. But the long arguments have to stay separate. You can type

```
$ ls -aF --color
```

to get a listing of all files including hidden files, with both color and extra characters used to denote directories and executable files. But a command like

```
$ ls -aFcolor
```

will produce strange results. (The fact that it produces any result at all might actually be a bug in Bash, but I can't swear to it.) **Don't** try to combine long options like this.

You can also mark the end of the argument list by adding an argument of '--' (two hyphens).

It is worth noting that the single-letter arguments to commands were the original

UNIX standard, but it was a pretty non-standard standard, since the authors of every utility chose their own argument names, often without regard to other existing utilities. The trend under Linux has been to encourage the use of the more user-friendly long arguments, and to encourage standardization of some of the argument names. For example, many utilities use the short form argument '-h' to mean 'help,' and may support the long-form version '--help' as well. It is also common to see the short option '-v' used to request the version number of a program, or its longer form '--version.' Some utilities support both sets of options, while others may support only one. For example, to see the version number of the ls command, you must type

```
$ ls --version
ls (fileutils) 4.1
Written by Richard Stallman and David MacKenzie.

Copyright (C) 2001 Free Software Foundation, Inc.
This is free software; see the source for copying
conditions. There is NO
warranty; not even for MERCHANTABILITY or FITNESS FOR A
PARTICULAR PURPOSE.

$ ls -v
```

will also give output, but here the '-v' means something different from the program's version number.

Unfortunately, you will still find many commands that use different argument names for similar functionality.

GNU Utilities: The Hidden Bonus of the Git Bash Shell

We have mentioned that Bash makes use of both built-in commands and external commands. The built-in commands are part of the code that implements Bash itself, but where do we find its external commands?

On UNIX and Linux, external commands are found in specific directories like /bin (for regular utilities), /sbin (for administrative utilities), and several others. These tools are considered part of the operating system, and ship with every Linux distribution.

In the case of Git running on Windows, the external commands are installed as part of the Git application. These external commands are collectively known as the GNU utilities. 'GNU' is a recursive acronym meaning 'GNU is Not UNIX.' (Computer scientists are devious people.) These utilities were originally created by Richard Stallman and the Free Software Foundation as part of an open source implementation of UNIX. While the GNU operating system never really took off, the GNU utilities were incorporated into Linux and survive to this day as vital tools for Linux users. The Git installation provides a subset of these tools that are useful for building the Git software from source code, but you and I can use them for our own purposes as well.

Where are These Utilities Really Located?

The external commands for the Git Bash shell can be found in the directory

```
C:\Program Files (x86)\Git\bin
```

assuming you installed Git in the default location. You can confirm that this is the right directory by right-clicking on the 'Git Bash' icon and choosing the 'Properties' menu. Look at the 'Target' entry to see the directory from which the Git Bash shell is started.

In Bash, type

```
$ cd "/c/Program Files (x86)/Git/bin"
```

to get to the correct location. For convenience, Git also provides you with a virtual directory name. You can type

```
$ cd /bin
```

to get the same result, even though Windows doesn't really have a /bin directory. Once you are there, type 'ls *.exe' to see most of the executable files that are present:

```
$ ls *.exe
antiword.exe    env.exe              gzip.exe      pdftotext.exe      ssh.exe
basename.exe    expr.exe             hd2u.exe      perl.exe           tail.exe
bash.exe        false.exe            head.exe      ps.exe             tar.exe
bison.exe       find.exe             iconv.exe     rebase.exe         tclsh.exe
bzip2.exe       flex.exe             id.exe        rm.exe             tclsh85.exe
cat.exe         gawk.exe             kill.exe      rmdir.exe          tee.exe
chmod.exe       getcp.exe            less.exe      rxvt.exe           touch.exe
cmp.exe         git.exe              ln.exe        scp.exe            tr.exe
connect.exe     gpg.exe              ls.exe        sed.exe            true.exe
cp.exe          gpgkeys_curl.exe     m4.exe        sh.exe             uname.exe
curl.exe        gpgkeys_finger.exe   md5sum.exe    sleep.exe          uniq.exe
cut.exe         gpgkeys_hkp.exe      mkdir.exe     sort.exe           unzip.exe
date.exe        gpgkeys_ldap.exe     msmtp.exe     split.exe          wc.exe
diff.exe        gpgsplit.exe         mv.exe        ssh-add.exe        wish.exe
dirname.exe     gpgv.exe             openssl.exe   ssh-agent.exe      wish85.exe
dos2unix.exe    grep.exe             patch.exe     ssh-keygen.exe     xargs.exe
du.exe          gunzip.exe           pdfinfo.exe   ssh-keyscan.exe
```

There are 84 such utilities present (including the whole Perl programming language), yet the Git documentation barely mentions their existence! While this is only a small subset of the utilities included in a typical Linux distribution, it is enough to make it relatively easy to do software development work in a Windows environment.

But wait, there's more! There are an additional 19 utilities not implemented as .exe files, including a full implementation of the popular Vim editor (though only the non-GUI version of Vim):

```
astextplain
awk
bunzip2
c_rehash
clear
docx2txt
echo
egrep
gitk
gpg-zip
gunzip
printf
pwd
```

```
recodetree
start
vi
vim
which
yacc
```

These additional utilities are implemented in a variety of ways. Several are just shortcuts for referring to other utilities. For example, 'awk' refers to the GNU implementation of the Awk text processing language (a predecessor to Perl), known as 'gawk.' The GNU implementation has more features than the original Awk. (Most GNU utilities have additional features and command-line arguments compared to the original UNIX utility they were based on.)

Some of the other utilities in the second list are implemented as shell scripts or even cmd.exe batch files. There are also a few utilities that were implemented as Perl scripts. For example, the docx2txt Perl script grabs all the text from a Word .docx file by stripping out all the formatting codes.

Note that not all of the utilities provided by Git were part of the GNU project. For example, Vim is a clone of the original UNIX vi editor, developed by Bram Moolenaar (and which provided many additional features beyond the original vi). The Perl programming language was developed by Larry Wall and generously given to the world.

As a user of these commands, you don't normally care how they are implemented; you just want to know that they are available. But how do you use them? First, many of the commands accept the '--help' option. For example,

```
$ ls --help
```

displays a couple of screen pages' worth of command-line options. If this isn't sufficient for your needs, there is plenty of help available on the Internet. On a UNIX or Linux system, the traditional way to learn about operating system commands is by using the 'man' command to look up their manual pages. However, the 'man' command is not included with the Git software. (It would be useless without having all the documentation files as well.) This isn't a big concern, as you can simply type a phrase like

```
ls man page
```

into your favorite search engine (such as Google; ixquick.com and duckduckgo.com are good choices for those who don't want Google tracking everything they look at). Just keep in mind that some of the GNU utilities provided by Git are not the latest and greatest versions included in Linux distributions, so not all the options listed on a man page may be accurate for every command. (Surprisingly, as of this writing, the Bash shell provided with Git 1.9.0 is only version 3.1.0, even though Bash 4.2 is used on most Linux distributions!)

We'll give an overview of many of the included utilities as we continue our discussion of Git Bash, but if you need more information, there are many detailed tutorials for any given utility available on the Internet.

Shell File Globbing

When Bash reads a command line, it breaks up or **tokenizes** the line into pieces separated by spaces, and tries to identify the pieces. The first element is always an executable command (which might be a shell builtin or an external command like a Bash script). The rest of the line is broken up into command-line options (recognizable by the single or double hyphen preceding them), I/O redirection symbols (which we'll discuss in a later section), and file names or directory paths. When Bash sees a string that it interprets as a file name, it looks for any special characters that may be embedded in it and performs **file name expansion** or **globbing.** When used as arguments to Bash commands, file names may contain **wildcard characters** and **character classes.** We'll start by listing what these special characters mean and then show some examples using our old friend the ls command.

Shell File Globbing Wildcards	
*	Wildcard that matches any number of characters
?	Wildcard that matches exactly one character

Shell Character Class Notation	
[]	Defines a character class containing letters, numbers, or other symbols; e.g., '[Aa]' matches uppercase 'A' or lowercase 'a'
-	The hyphen character is used to define a range of characters in a character class, such as '[0-9]' to match a single digit
^	The caret or circumflex negates the characters listed in a character class (if it is at the start of the class)

Note that a character class defines the possible values that can be used to match *a single character*. For example, '[A-Z]' will match any single uppercase character. We'll see examples of this shortly.

Let's try out the special characters that can be used for file name expansions:

```
$ cd /bin
```

```
$ ls *.exe
antiword.exe    env.exe                gzip.exe       pdftotext.exe     ssh.exe
basename.exe    expr.exe               hd2u.exe       perl.exe          tail.exe
bash.exe        false.exe              head.exe       ps.exe            tar.exe
bison.exe       find.exe               iconv.exe      rebase.exe        tclsh.exe
bzip2.exe       flex.exe               id.exe         rm.exe            tclsh85.exe
cat.exe         gawk.exe               kill.exe       rmdir.exe         tee.exe
chmod.exe       getcp.exe              less.exe       rxvt.exe          touch.exe
cmp.exe         git.exe                ln.exe         scp.exe           tr.exe
connect.exe     gpg.exe                ls.exe         sed.exe           true.exe
cp.exe          gpgkeys_curl.exe       m4.exe         sh.exe            uname.exe
curl.exe        gpgkeys_finger.exe     md5sum.exe     sleep.exe         uniq.exe
cut.exe         gpgkeys_hkp.exe        mkdir.exe      sort.exe          unzip.exe
date.exe        gpgkeys_ldap.exe       msmtp.exe      split.exe         wc.exe
diff.exe        gpgsplit.exe           mv.exe         ssh-add.exe       wish.exe
dirname.exe     gpgv.exe               openssl.exe    ssh-agent.exe     wish85.exe
dos2unix.exe    grep.exe               patch.exe      ssh-keygen.exe    xargs.exe
du.exe          gunzip.exe             pdfinfo.exe    ssh-keyscan.exe
```

Match all files starting with 'g' and ending with 'zip:'

```
$ ls g*zip.exe
gunzip.exe   gzip.exe
```

Match all files starting with any characters but ending with 'zip:'

```
$ ls *zip*.exe
bzip2.exe  gunzip.exe  gzip.exe  unzip.exe
```

Match all six-character file names that begin with 'l' and end with the '.exe' extension. (Also, the -F option appends an asterisk to the file names matched, showing that they are both executable files.)

```
$ ls -F l?.exe
ln.exe*  ls.exe*
```

Notice in the next two examples that '*' can match zero characters, while '?' has to match exactly one:

```
$ ls vi*
vi  vim
```

```
$ ls vi?
vim
```

Now let's try out some character classes. If we only want to look at file names that include hyphens or underscores, we can use an expression like

```
$ ls *[_-]*
c_rehash              libintl-8.dll           libsvn_swig_perl-1-
0.dll
curl-ca-bundle.crt    libneon-25.dll          libsvn_wc-1-0.dll
gpg-zip               libpoppler-7.dll        msys-1.0.dll
gpgkeys_curl.exe      libsvn_client-1-0.dll   msys-crypto-0.9.8.dll
gpgkeys_finger.exe    libsvn_delta-1-0.dll    msys-minires.dll
gpgkeys_hkp.exe       libsvn_diff-1-0.dll     msys-perl5_8.dll
gpgkeys_ldap.exe      libsvn_fs-1-0.dll       msys-regex-1.dll
libapr-0-0.dll        libsvn_fs_fs-1-0.dll    msys-ssl-0.9.8.dll
libaprutil-0-0.dll    libsvn_ra-1-0.dll       msys-z.dll
libcurl-4.dll         libsvn_ra_dav-1-0.dll   msysltdl-3.dll
libexpat-0.dll        libsvn_ra_local-1-0.dll ssh-add.exe
libgsasl-7.def        libsvn_ra_svn-1-0.dll   ssh-agent.exe
libgsasl-7.dll        libsvn_repos-1-0.dll    ssh-keygen.exe
libiconv-2.dll        libsvn_subr-1-0.dll     ssh-keyscan.exe
```

The above expression says to look for files starting with any characters, followed by at least one underscore or hyphen, followed by any characters.

If you want only files that contain at least one uppercase letter in their names, try

```
$ ls *[A-Z]*
libW11.dll  pthreadGC2.dll
```

If you want the names of .dll files that have exactly two digits before the file extension, do

```
$ ls *[0-9][0-9].dll
libW11.dll  libneon-25.dll  tcl85.dll  tclpip85.dll
tk85.dll
```

If you want files that *don't* start with any lowercase letter before 'x,' do

```
$ ls [^a-w]*
xargs.exe  yacc
```

With the files in /bin, you could also get the same result by typing

```
$ ls [x-z]*
xargs.exe  yacc
```

However, the last two commands are not really equivalent in the general case. The first command would also list any file names that begin with an uppercase letter (or any other legal character for a file name except the lowercase letters listed). Because there aren't any such files in the /bin directory, the second command produces the same result. There are often multiple ways to find a particular set of files via file name expansion, just keep in mind that two glob expressions may not be as equivalent as you thought they were.

It is important to note that file globs will *not* match the 'hidden' dot files that start with a period. Bash itself has such files hidden in your home directory, but you have to be careful how you look for them:

```
$ cd

$ ls *bash
ls: *bash: No such file or directory
```

```
$ ls .b*
.bash_history   .bashrc
```

Now that you understand how file name expansion works, you'll see that it can also be applied to other commands that also expect file names. Examples of this are the 'rm' command for removing files, and the 'rmdir' command for removing directories..

But before we can remove files or directories, we first have to create them! Directories can be created easily with the 'mkdir' command. Let's assume for this exercise that you wanted to create a Web application using the CodeIgniter framework for the PHP language. Using this framework, each Web page is represented as a view file written in PHP. We won't worry about the other directories used by the framework; for now, let's just create a views directory in your home directory:

```
$ cd
```

```
$ mkdir views
```

```
$ cd views
```

Now we need to create the files representing each Web page. Let's assume that we are creating a small application to sell several of the most common brands of digital cameras. We could create each file by opening a text editor, typing in some text, and saving the file, but that is very tedious when we just want some quick (and empty) files to experiment with. This is such a common operation that UNIX provided a utility specifically for creating empty 'placeholder' files, called the 'touch' command. (Applying this command to existing files updates their access and modification times to the current time; applying the command to a non-existent file creates a new empty file whose access and modification times are set to the current time.) Create some PHP Web page files with the following commands:

```
$ touch index.hmtl home.php about.php contact_us.php
site_map.php help.php
```

```
$ touch canon1.php canon2.php
```

```
$ touch nikon1.php nikon2.php nikon3.php
```

```
$ touch panasonic1.php panasonic2.php
```

```
$ touch samsung1.php samsung2.php samsung3.php
samsung4.php samsung5.php

$ touch sony1.php sony2.php sony3.php
```

Note that the 'touch' command silently creates new files when the specified files don't exist. Since we're only creating empty files for this exercise, you don't need to worry about writing any PHP code. You should see a directory listing like this:

```
$ ls
about.php         help.php      nikon3.php        samsung2.php
site_map.php
canon1.php        home.php      panasonic1.php    samsung3.php    sony1.php
canon2.php        nikon1.php    panasonic2.php    samsung4.php    sony2.php
contact_us.php    nikon2.php    samsung1.php      samsung5.php    sony3.php
```

If you decide to sell fewer Samsung cameras, you might want to eliminate pages four and five of Samsung products:

```
$ rm samsung[45].php
```

```
$ ls
about.php     contact_us.php  nikon1.php  panasonic1.php  samsung2.php  sony1.php
canon1.php    help.php        nikon2.php  panasonic2.php  samsung3.php  sony2.php
canon2.php    home.php        nikon3.php  samsung1.php    site_map.php  sony3.php
```

Note that in this example the character class '[45]' refers to a single character that could have the value '4' or '5.' We could have achieved the same result by using a character class range:

```
$ rm samsung[4-5].php
```

If Sony cameras are selling poorly, we might decide to remove all the Sony pages entiresly:

```
$ rm sony*.php
```

```
$ ls
about.php     contact_us.php  nikon1.php  panasonic1.php  samsung2.php
canon1.php    help.php        nikon2.php  panasonic2.php  samsung3.php
canon2.php    home.php        nikon3.php  samsung1.php    site_map.php
```

```
```

We could have achieved the same result with the command

```
$ rm sony?.php
```

But if we had had twenty pages of Sony cameras (with file names ranging up to sony20.php), this command would have only eliminated the single-digit pages. We could also have achieved the same result by specifically removing the three pages of interest:

```
$ rm sony[1-3].php
```

But the previous two expressions are more compact and easier to type.

You should always be careful when removing multiple files simultaneously; if you get the file globbing expression wrong, you might eliminate more files than you intended. Making it easy to recover from accidents like this is why source control systems like Git were invented. However, the 'rm' command itself provides a built-in way to avoid accidents: use the '-i' option, which prompts you for each file that you want to remove. If we inadvertently give a command to remove all Nikon pages when we really intended to keep the first page of Nikon products, the '-i' option will give us another chance to avoid disaster:

```
$ rm -i nikon?.php
rm: remove `nikon1.php'? n
rm: remove `nikon2.php'? y
rm: remove `nikon3.php'? Y
```

Your response can be an uppercase or lowercase 'y' or 'n.'

```
$ ls
about.php    contact_us.php   nikon1.php      samsung1.php
site_map.php
canon1.php   help.php         panasonic1.php  samsung2.php
canon2.php   home.php         panasonic2.php  samsung3.php
```

If you like to live dangerously, you can type

```
$ rm *
```

to remove **all** of the files in the current directory. Be sure that you know where you are and what files are present before you issue such a command! Or use the '-i' option.

Once all the files are gone, we can remove the directory they were in by moving to the parent directory with the

```
$ cd ..
```

command. The two dots are a special shorthand for referring to the directory above the current directory. (A single dot refers to the current directory.) Once we are in the right location, we can confirm that views is indeed a directory with a command like

```
$ ls -Fd views
views/
```

Now remove the directory with the command

```
rmdir views
```

We could have achieved the same results in one step by returning to your home directory and using additional options for the 'rm' command:

```
$ cd
```

```
$ rm -rf views
```

The '-r' option recursively removes all files and subdirectories (and the files in the subdirectories). The '-f' option forces removal of all files without prompting. Note that these are *very* dangerous options! A foolish person with administrative privileges could issue commands like

```
$ cd /c
```

```
$ rm -rf *
```

This will destroy the entire contents of your C: drive! There is no way to undo such a command (though you could at least interrupt it with <Ctrl-c> before it has a chance to delete everything). The only way to recover is if you have a complete backup of your drive contents. **Never** issue such a command when you are being distracted by other things. Always look carefully at the directory contents and confirm which directory you are in before you use such a command. The incredible efficiency of UNIX-style commands can destroy months or years of work if you are not careful.

Since we have spent some time talking about file creation and destruction, I should mention that you can also rename or move files with the 'mv' command. For example,

```
$ mv mispelled_file.txt properly_spelled_file.txt
```

You can also move a set of files to another directory. If you wanted to move all .txt files in the current directory to a different directory, use the following syntax:

```
$ mv *.txt another_directory
```

In a simlar fashion, you can copy files with the 'cp' command. For example, it is trivial to make a backup of one of your files:

```
$ cp my_important_file.txt my_important_file.bak
```

As with the 'rm' command, there is a '-i' or '--interactive' option available to prevent you from overwriting an existing file when you make a copy. You can of course copy a file to another directory instead:

```
$ cp my_important_file.txt another_directory
```

You can also recursively copy an entire directory hierarchy to another directory using the '-r' option:

```
$ cp -r primary_archive/* backup_archive
```

The directory you want to copy to must already exist; if it doesn't, you'll get an error message like

```
$ cp -r primary_archive/* backup_archive
cp: copying multiple files, but last argument
`backup_archive' is not a directory
Try `cp --help' for more information.
```

In this case, first do

```
$ mkdir backup_archive
```

and then do the copy command again. Note also that our copy command copies the *contents* of primary_archive by using the syntax 'primary_archive/*.' If you don't include the '/*,' what you will end up with is a copy of the primary_archive directory under backup_archive, and then the contents of primary_archive below that. That is, you'll end up with a backup directory structure that looks like 'backup_archive/primary_archive.' This is usually *not* what you want.

There are a couple of other options to the 'cp' command that can be very handy when doing mass copies, as shown by 'cp --help:'

```
-p, --preserve            preserve file attributes if possible
-u, --update              copy only when the SOURCE file is newer
                            than the destination file or when the
                            destination file is missing
```

For example, if you want to make regular backups of a directory, you could use a command like

```
$ cp -rpu primary_archive/* backup_archive
```

One other common command that I should mention in this section is the 'cat' command. This command is not related to felines. Instead, the purpose of the command is to con**cat**enate multiple (plain text) files into one large file. For example, if you are writing the outline of a book, you might divide the information about the book into separate files like

```
table_of_contents.txt
book_body.txt
appendices.txt
```

If you later decide to combine all of these files into a single text file (maybe you want to e-mail it to a friend as a single attachment), you could use the command

```
$ cat table_of_contents.txt book_body.txt appendices.txt
> entire_outline.txt
```

(The 'greater than' symbol tells Bash to save the result of the concatenation to an output file named 'entire_outline.txt.' This is an example of I/O redirection, which we'll discuss after the next section.)

Surprisingly, 'cat' even allows you to create brand new files from the keyboard, without having to use a text editor! Type the full command first, and then type in as much text as you want. Then hit <Enter> to start a new line and press <Ctrl-d>. This ends text entry, and once again the '>' symbol will send all the material you typed to the specified output file. If you are writing company documentation, you might want to create a simple copyright notice that can be easily incorporated into other files. Here's how:

```
$ cat > copyright.txt
Copyright 2014 Faceless Conglomerate Inc.
<Ctrl-d>
```

Once the file has been created, you can view its contents with the command

```
$ cat copyright.txt
Copyright 2014 Faceless Conglomerate Inc.
```

The default action of the cat command is to display its output to the screen. This means that if you do the 'cat' command on a single file (as above), its contents will be displayed in a fashion very similar to that of the traditional DOS 'TYPE' command. This works great for a file with only a few lines of text, but what if you have a really long file?

There is a solution for that too; namely, the GNU 'less' utility. This command is what UNIX refers to as a 'pager' program, meaning that it will display the contents of a file one screen page at a time. To use it, pick a longer file and type a command like

```
$ less my_long_file.txt
```

If the file is less than one screen page in length, the command will work like 'cat' and simply display everything at once. If the file is longer, you will see the file name at the bottom of the window. To see the next page, simply press the space bar once. This lets you scroll through the file one page at a time, but 'less' has more power than this. Once you get beyond the first page, you can scroll backward by hitting the letter 'b' instead of the space bar. But wait, there's more! You can also *search* for a particular line in the file. Press '/' (a forward slash character) and then enter the search string and hit <Enter> to search forward in the file. To search backward from the present location, do the same thing, except start by hitting the '?' (question mark) key. Hit the 'q' or 'Q' key to quit displaying the file and return to the Bash prompt. To summarize,

Basic Command Options for the Less Utility	
\<Space\>	Scroll forward one screen page at a time
b	Scroll backward one screen page at a time
/search_string	Search forward for the search_string
?search_string	Search backward for the search_string
q or Q	Quit displaying the file and return to the Bash prompt

Note that you can apply this command to multiple files at once, so if you have files like

```
long_file1.txt
long_file2.txt
```

you can type the command

```
$ less long_file?.txt
```

and 'less' will successively display the contents of both files. Less is actually loaded with features. Many (but not all) of its commands are compatible with the vi editor, so if you know vi, you'll feel right at home. You can see the nicely organized list of features by typing

```
$ less --help
```

You may wonder why this program is called 'less.' The name is a pun on the first UNIX pager, called 'more.' The original program could only move forward in the file, whereas 'less' lets you go backward as well. So the name of the program almost makes sense, more or less. ☺

How to Find Things

We have seen that it is easy to use shell file globbing to apply a command to a specific set of files. However, many people who work on large projects or multiple small projects end up with thousands of files scattered across dozens if not hundreds of directories. Just keeping track of where all your files are can quickly become a mess. This is where another GNU utility, the 'find' command, comes to the rescue.

The 'find' command has many useful features, but the basic form of the command is

```
$ find starting_directory file_name_spec action
```

As an example, suppose you want to find all the PDF files in your account. You could do this with commands like

```
$ cd
$ find . -name "*.pdf" -print
```

The cd command returns you to your home directory before starting the search. The dot after the find command is Bash-speak for the current directory; it means "start searching for the specified files in the current directory." The files to search for are specified by the '-name' option, and the file specification is enclosed in quotes to prevent the '*' wildcard character from being directly interpreted by Bash (although it is the same type of file glob used by Bash, we want this file glob to be expanded by the find utility itself). The '-print' option prints out each file found that matches the required specification. Printing the found file names is the default action of find, so the '-print' option is not strictly necessary. I'm in the habit of using it anyway, since there was once a time that this option was required.

Note that by default find searches for files starting in the starting_directory, and *continuing in all subdirectories* of the starting_directory. It doesn't stop when the first requested file is found; it keeps going until it has examined all files in all of the subdirectories, so that it can return the maximum number of files that match the requested specification. The path to each file found is reported on a separate line of output.

If find can use an arbitrary starting directory, you may wonder why we bothered to cd to our home directory before starting the search. The answer is, you don't have to do this. On Linux systems, it is common to search the whole computer for files. In this case, you would use a command like

```
$ find / -name "*.pdf" -print
```

The forward slash tells find to start at the root level of the entire file system. However, **this syntax does not work the same way in the Git Bash shell on Windows!** Instead, '/' is a virtual directory like /bin which represents the location where Git was installed; namely,

```
/c/Program Files (x86)/Git
```

So if you use the forward slash as your starting directory, find will start its search in
the location where Git was installed. This is probably not what you want, unless you
are looking specifically for files included with Git. Instead, if you want to search for
files in your own account, use Bash's '~' character to represent your home directory.
For example, to find your .bashrc file, use the command

```
$ find ~ -name ".bashrc" -print
/e/Users/Michael Hanna/.bashrc
```

You probably only have one copy of your .bashrc file, but if there are a lot of files in
your account, you'll notice that your hard disk keeps grinding away as find searches
every subdirectory for copies of the same file. If you already found what you wanted,
you can interrupt the search in mid-stream by typing <Ctrl-c>.

If you want to restrict find to searching just the starting directory, you can also use the
'-maxdepth' option to tell how many levels to go down in the directory hierarchy:

```
$ find ~ -maxdepth 1 -name ".bashrc" -print
/e/Users/Michael Hanna/.bashrc
```

If you want to search whole drives for files, just give the Bash-style drive name as the
starting directory:

```
$ find /c -name "*.txt" -print
```

If you have multiple drive partitions, you can list them at the start of the find
command, and find will search each directory hierarchy in succession:

```
$ find /c /e -name "*.txt" -print
```

Note that you may get 'permission denied' errors if find tries to examine files that you
do not have permission to read. This is likely to happen if you search a whole drive
and your Git Bash window was not run with administrator privileges.

If you wanted to search for all Microsoft Word files in the current directory, you could
use a command like this

```
$ find . -name "*.doc*" -print
```

which will find all .doc and .docx files, as well as any other files whose extension begins with the '.doc' string. A more accurate way to get only the files you want would be to type

```
$ find . \( -name '*.doc' -o -name '*.docx' \) -print
```

Here we are searching for files whose extension is either '.doc' or '.docx.' The '-o' options serves as a logical OR operator. The conditions that we are OR-ing are surrounded by parentheses. The parentheses have to be escaped (with backslashes or quotes); otherwise, Bash will think you are trying to start a subshell. Note that you must have at least one space between the opening parenthesis and the first item after it, and between the last item and the closing parenthesis. If you don't do this, find will barf up an error because it can't interpret its arguments properly:

```
$ find . \(-name '*.doc' -o -name '*.docx'\) -print
find: invalid predicate `(-name'
```

Note that there is no direct logical AND operator. Instead, you just chain multiple (space-separated) conditions together, and find will match the files that match *all* of the requirements. Find also lets you negate expressions by preceding them with an exclamation point. (Be sure to have at least one space surrounding the exclamation point.) For example, if you want to find all the files in your account that *aren't* PDF files, you could do this:

```
$ find ~ ! -name "*.pdf" -print
```

Find doesn't have to only operate on files; it can operate on directories as well by use of the '-type' option. Typical values for this option are '-type f' for files (the default behavior) or '-type d' for directory. Linux system users can also look for other types of files like symbolic links. If you wanted to search for all directory names beginning with 'Program Files' on the C:\ drive, you would type

```
$ find /c -name "Program Files*" -type d -print
```

which would produce

```
/c/Program Files
/c/Program Files (x86)
```

along with some 'permission denied' errors.

Find has other actions available besides simply printing each file name. For example, there is an '-ls' option to list each file name in a manner similar to the ls command. This is mainly used to verify that find is finding the files that you want, in preparation for taking some other action, such as deleting them. If you do a lot of C or C++ programming, for example, you may periodically get core dumps, which will leave files named 'core' in your development directories. You can search for these files with a command like

```
$ find ~ -name "core" -ls
```

Once you have confirmed that you are finding the right set of files, you can then use the '-exec' option to invoke the rm command on each file found:

```
$ find ~ -name "core" -exec rm {} \;
```

The '-exec' option must be followed by the name of a simple command. The file that the command is to act on is represented by the pair of curly braces ('{}'). Note that whatever command you give must be terminated by an escaped semicolon (and there must be a space in front of it as well). If you don't terminate the command properly, you'll get an error like this:

```
$ find ~ -name "core" -exec rm {}
find: missing argument to `-exec'
```

Be very careful if you decide to remove files with the find utility. If you remove the wrong files, there is no way to get them back unless you either a) have backup copies, or b) you stored the files in a version control system like Git.

You can also use the '-exec' option for less dangerous operations, such as using egrep to look for strings in the files that are found. (There will be more coverage of this command in the next section.) For example, suppose you are writing code in Ruby and you want to find all the function definitions in your Ruby source files (which end with a '.rb' extension). Then you could use a find command like

```
$ find . -name "*.rb" -print -exec egrep 'def ' {} \;
./cookbook/app/controllers/application.rb
./cookbook/app/controllers/categories_controller.rb
  def index
```

```
def show
def new
def edit
def create
def update
def destroy
.
.
.
```

In this case, egrep is followed by the string to search for (all Ruby function definitions start with the keyword 'def'), and then the pair of curly braces that represents the file to search. One oddity you may have noticed about the above command is that we used the '-print' action as well as the '-exec' action. The reason for this is that we want to be told in which file each function definition was found. If you do the above command without the '-print' option, you'll still see the function definitions, but you won't know which files they are associated with! Not all possible combinations of command options will produce useful output.

We have covered only a tiny fraction of find's capabilities. Find can also find files by size, modification time, and many other criteria. Covering everything would use up half the space in this book and overwhelm you with too much detail. The GNU utilities are incredibly powerful, but you need to get comfortable with the most common ways of using them before trying to explore every obscure option.

Regular Expressions and grep

A topic closely related to shell file globbing is that of **regular expressions.** Globbing is done when Bash finds special characters in any piece of a command line that looks like a file name. Regular expressions use a similar (but not identical) notation to allow individual utilities to look for or edit particular patterns of text (which aren't necessarily file names). Bash itself only has limited regular expression capability. (Actually, Bash version 3.0 or greater is supposed to have pretty good capability, but much of the functionality that I tried appeared to be broken on both Windows and Linux platforms, so I won't cover it here.)

Entire books have been written on the subject of regular expressions. Some of these books may give the misleading impression that there is one standard notation for regular expressions. Sadly, there isn't. Historically, each individual UNIX utility that supported regular expressions (and not all of them do) defined its own set of expressions. Early UNIX utilities only supported a very limited set of expressions.

When Larry Wall created the Perl programming language, he included the ability for the language to process a much richer set of regular expressions, and because Perl was ported to many other operating systems, it brought the power of regular expressions to operating systems that otherwise didn't support them at all. Many other programming languages (such as Ruby, Python, and PHP) have adopted Larry Wall's notation or something very similar to it. These languages provide what they call 'PCRE' or 'Perl-Compatible Regular Expressions.' This is a much more complex subject that we won't try to cover here, but you should be aware that many modern programming languages and text editors provide incredibly sophisticated ways for you to slice and dice text. The Perl regular expression library is probably the closest thing to a regular expression standard that currently exists.

However, even the limited regular expressions of common UNIX utilities provided much more power than those of other operating systems. We will demonstrate that here with the classic 'grep' utility, and its (formerly) more capable companion, 'egrep.' What do these rather strangely-named utilities do? They allow you to search for text in files. These could be plain text files of your latest poetry, or files written in any programming language. (Like all standard UNIX utilities, grep only works with plain text files. If you want to search a Microsoft Word document, for example, you'll also need to use something like the docx2txt command that we mentioned earlier to extract the text and then pass it to grep.)

'GREP' was originally an acronym for 'global regular expression print.' If the program had been written by mere mortals instead of computer scientists, it might have been called something more intuitive like 'search' or 'find_strings.' Searching for text strings in files is the primary mission for grep. When it finds a string that matches the regular expression, it returns *the entire line that contains that string.* So for a line that contains multiple copies of the string you want to match, you'll only get one line of output.

The basic regular expressions supported by many UNIX utilities used almost the same notation as that used for shell file globbing. The primary difference is that regular expressions use a period or dot as a wildcard for a single character, while the shell uses a question mark to represent a single character. If you keep this distinction in mind, you can already use regular expressions to search for basic text patterns with grep.

You call grep with syntax of the form

```
grep [OPTION]... PATTERN [FILE] …
```

(This is the usage message presented by the command 'grep --help.')

To take a concrete example, if you are a programmer writing code in the C language, you might want to search your source files to see what other files you are including with the '#include' command of the C preprocessor. You could find the include files used by all the C source files in your current directory with the command

```
$ grep '#include' *.c
```

Here, '#include' is a regular expression that simply asks grep to find that literal text. On the other hand, '*.c' is the list of files to search. This is *not* a regular expression; it is a shell file glob. When Bash sees this glob expression, it will replace it with a list of all files that end with the '.c' extension. When you search for literal characters with grep, the search pattern doesn't really need to be enclosed in quotation marks. But it is good to get into the habit of enclosing the search pattern in single quotes, as this will protect any special characters in the pattern from being interpreted (and replaced) by Bash.

A slightly more challenging example would be to search for references to the word 'cat' in a text file. Suppose our text file looks like this:

```
$ cat kitties.txt
When the cat's away, the mice will play.
Two cats are better than one cat.
My youngest cat quickly becomes thoroughly
catatonic and listless after
eating a big bowl of catnip.

Cat is a GNU utility that is rarely used by
the cats in my neighborhood.
```

Let's search for both uppercase and lowercase versions of 'cat.'

```
$ grep '[Cc]at' kitties.txt
When the cat's away, the mice will play.
```

```
Two cats are better than one cat.
My youngest cat quickly becomes thoroughly
catatonic and listless after
eating a big bowl of catnip.
Cat is a GNU utility that is rarely used by
the cats in my neighborhood.
```

This set of results might be a little different from what you were expecting. Note that grep returned lines in which the word 'cat' was embedded in another word like 'catatonic' or 'catnip.' One simple way to eliminate lines with 'cat' in embedded words is to include a space at the end of the search string:

```
$ grep '[Cc]at ' kitties.txt
My youngest cat quickly becomes thoroughly
Cat is a GNU utility that is rarely used by
```

Now we get far fewer results, but some of the text we might want is not included. We're missing references to "cat's" (with an apostrophe), as well as 'cats,' the plural of cats. We'll learn how to deal with cases like this after we cover the additional regular expression capability of grep. As we did with shell file globbing, we'll start by listing the regular expressions that grep supports and then show some examples of how to use them.

Unfortunately, the regular expressions used by grep are kind of a mess. It helps to understand that there have been a variety of grep implementations. The first and most limited one was 'grep.' Another popular implementation was 'egrep' or 'extended grep.' This provided a couple of additional regular expression notations that were not supported by the original grep.

The GNU grep project decided to give you the best of both worlds by providing identical regular expression capabilities to both grep and egrep. However, grep requires that several of the regular expression metacharacters have to be escaped by a backslash character. Egrep allows you to use those characters in your search string *without* escaping them. This is a needlessly confusing mess, especially since 'egrep' is actually implemented simply by calling grep with the '-E' or 'extended' option. Why not simply create identical regular expressions for both, and perhaps eliminate egrep entirely? That opportunity was missed, so you'll have to look at the tables below to know which notations you can use with grep versus egrep. To minimize typing, I recommend using egrep (whose expressions are shown in the middle column of the tables), and we'll use that for our later examples.

Single Character Regular Expressions

grep	grep -E/egrep	Meaning
a	a	Any single literal character
.	.	Match any single character
[]	[]	Match any character in the class
[^]	[^]	Match any character *not* in the class
a|b	a|b	Match either a or b

Regular Expression Grouping and Alternation

grep	grep -E/egrep	Meaning
\(expression\)	(expression)	Match the expression and create a backreference
\(expression1 \\| expression2 \)	(expression1 | expression2)	Match either expression and create a backreference

Multi-Character Regular Expressions

grep	grep -E/egrep	Meaning
a\?	a?	Match preceding term zero or one times
a*	a*	Match preceding term zero or more times
a\+	a+	Match preceding term one or more times
\{m\}	{m}	Match preceding term exactly m times
\{m,\}	{m,}	Match preceding term m or more times
\{,n\}	{,n}	Match preceding term at most n times
\{m,n\}	{m,n}	Match preceding term at least m times, but no more than n times

POSIX Bracket Expressions

(These expressions are intended for use inside a character class, so they need to be enclosed in another pair of square brackets.)

grep	grep -E/egrep	Meaning
[:alnum:]	[:alnum:]	Alphanumeric characters
[:alpha:]	[:alpha:]	Alphabetic characters
[:blank:]	[:blank:]	Spaces or tabs
[:cntrl:]	[:cntrl:]	Control characters
[:digit:]	[:digit:]	Digits
[:graph:]	[:graph:]	Graphical characters
[:lower:]	[:lower:]	Lowercase characters
[:print:]	[:print:]	Printable characters
[:punct:]	[:punct:]	Punctuation characters
[:space:]	[:space:]	Space, tab, newline, vertical tab, form feed, and carriage return
[:upper:]	[:upper:]	Uppercase characters
[:xdigit:]	[:xdigit:]	Hexadecimal digits

Special Characters for Word and Space Matching		
grep	**grep -E/egrep**	**Meaning**
\b	\b	Match empty string at the edge of a word
\B	\B	Match empty strings not at the edge of a word
\<	\<	Match empty string at beginning of word
\>	\>	Match empty string at end of word
\w	\w	Match word characters; equivalent to '[_[:alnum:]]'
\W	\W	Match non-word characters; equivalent to '[^_[:alnum:]]'
\s	\s	Match whitespace characters; equivalent to '[[:space:]]'
\S	\S	Match non-whitespace characters; equivalent to '[^[:space:]]'

There is quite a lot of information in the tables above, so don't feel you have to learn it all now. There is no need to memorize all this notation; just refer back to the tables whenever you need to create a more complex expression.

One thing we might like to do with our example file is to search for 'cat' as a separate word. This can be done by using the word boundary metacharacters '\<' and '\>:'

```
$ egrep '\<[Cc]at\>' kitties.txt
When the cat's away, the mice will play.
Two cats are better than one cat.
My youngest cat quickly becomes thoroughly
Cat is a GNU utility that is rarely used by
```

Even the apostrophe in "cat's" acts as a word boundary, so that instance of the word is matched. Note that even though we used egrep, the regular expression characters in the last table above still have to be preceded by a backslash. Otherwise, egrep will search for the word 'cat' surrounded by the '<' and '>' characters. There is no such line in this file, so you won't get any results:

```
$ egrep '<[Cc]at>' kitties.txt
```

Although I rarely use word boundary metacharacters in my own regular expressions, you can see that they occasionally come in handy.

Now let's try a bit more sophisticated example. Suppose that you have a file full of addresses, say, "addresses.txt,' and that you want to extract all the Zip codes from your file. How might we do this? First, we'll use some fictional data in a format similar to real addresses:

```
$ cat addresses.txt
Wherever
P.O. Box 993771
Durham, NC. 02331

Somewhere
334 Twit Terrace
Camden, NJ 32976-2813

Elsewhere
403 Road Kill Lane
Austin, TX. 84703
```

Clearly, we want all lines that include five digits in a row. (This requirement will also pick up nine-digit Zip codes as well.) The obvious way to do this is with syntax like

```
$ egrep '[0-9][0-9][0-9][0-9][0-9]' addresses.txt
P.O. Box 993771
Durham, NC. 02331
Camden, NJ 32976-2813
Austin, TX. 84703
```

This grabs all the lines with Zip codes, but also gets a number that isn't a Zip code. We'll solve this problem in a moment, but first let's consider how we could make our regular expression simpler, which will reduce the amount of typing and our chances of making errors. The table for 'Multi-Character Regular Expressions' shows that we can use the curly brace notation to specify exactly how many digits in a row we wish to match:

```
$ egrep '[0-9]{5}' addresses.txt
P.O. Box 993771
Durham, NC. 02331
Camden, NJ 32976-2813
Austin, TX. 84703
```

Note that even though '993771' has more than five digits, the last five digits of this number do match the regular expression, so egrep extracts the line anyway. (Regular expressions are considered to be **greedy** by default, meaning that they match text as far to the right as possible in a given line.) We could also have used a POSIX bracket expression to get the same result:

```
$ egrep '[[:digit:]]{5}' addresses.txt
P.O. Box 993771
Durham, NC. 02331
Camden, NJ 32976-2813
Austin, TX. 84703
```

Note the outer pair of square brackets that puts '[:digit:]' into a character class. If you try the same search with only a single pair of square brackets, the search will return nothing because it is looking for five occurrences in a row of the literal string '[:digit:].'

Now that we know how to make the expression a little simpler, let's solve the problem of getting search results we didn't want. We can see that in the format of this particular file, the city and state are listed on the same line as the Zip code. So let's make the two-character state code part of our regular expression:

```
$ egrep '[A-Z]{2}\s+[0-9]{5}' addresses.txt
```

This type of expression should work according to the documentation, but doesn't produce any results. The problem is that '\s' (which represents whitespace) isn't handled properly. The subexpression '\s+" should match at least one character of whitespace. That is, there needs to be at least one space between the two-character state code and the Zip code. Perhaps our version of GNU grep is too old to support this feature. When you discover problems like this in the real world, you can try to do a workaround. The '\s' notation is equivalent to the '[:space:]' POSIX bracket expression, so we can rewrite our regular expression as

```
$ egrep '[[:upper:]]{2}[[:space:]]+[[:digit:]]{5}' addresses.txt
Camden, NJ 32976-2813
```

This expression does produce some output. You are also free to mix POSIX and non-POSIX notation in the same regular expression:

```
$ egrep '[A-Z]{2}[[:space:]]+[0-9]{5}' addresses.txt
Camden, NJ 32976-2813
```

Both forms produced the same result, but that result shows only one of the three Zip codes in the file! What went wrong? If you look carefully at the file, you'll see that two of the state names are followed by a period. This is the proper form for an abbreviation, though the Postal Service seems to prefer state codes without periods. We want to extract the Zip codes regardless of how the state codes are written. This is easy to do:

```
$ egrep '[A-Z]{2}\.?[[:space:]]+[0-9]{5}' addresses.txt
Durham, NC. 02331
Camden, NJ 32976-2813
Austin, TX. 84703
```

We simply added an expression ('\.?') that matches zero or one periods after the two-character state code. Note that the period has to be escaped with a backslash; otherwise, it is considered a wildcard that will match *any* single character, not just a period.

We can now translate the whole rather intimidating-looking expression into English: "Match lines that have two uppercase characters, possibly followed by a period, followed by one or more spaces, followed by five digits." This expression correctly returns all the lines that contain Zip codes while ignoring the P.O. box number in one of the addresses.

Useful Options for grep

Grep has a variety of command line options that can help you with text searching tasks. I'll only list a few of the most commonly used ones here:

Command Line Options for grep	
-i	Case-insensitive search
-n	Print line number in file where string was found
-v	Invert the search; i.e., find all lines that *don't* match the pattern

Regular expressions can look strange to the uninitiated, but once you get some practice in using them, you will find them incredibly useful. They are used not only by programming languages and GNU-style utilities, but also by text editors and even word processors. (For example, LibreOffice Writer supports doing search-and-replace operations using many of the same regular expressions we just covered.) So don't let regular expressions intimidate you.

I/O Redirection and Pipes

So far we have learned about a few of the powerful GNU utilities included with the Git Bash shell. Now we are going to learn how to *combine* multiple commands and use them with external files as well. The UNIX philosophy was that each tool in the system should do one task well. The other key part of that philosophy is that the operating system should treat everything as if it were a file, even when it is talking to your keyboard or your printer. Even the configuration of UNIX and Linux systems emphasizes putting information into human-readable files. This makes it easy to slice and dice information when it is needed.

UNIX and Linux associate devices on your system with **file descriptors.** The most common file descriptors are stdin, stdout, and stderr (which are represented by the numbers 0, 1, and 2). These names are short for 'standard input,' 'standard output,' and 'standard error.' Standard input normally comes from your keyboard. Standard output normally goes to your terminal screen, as does standard error. One of the unusual features of UNIX and Linux is that they can treat error messages differently than normal output. If you save data to a file, you can save normal output, normal output plus error messages, or just the error messages alone. The choice is entirely up to you. What adds even more power to this design is the ability to connect the output of one program to the input of another program via a **pipe.** A pipe contains a stream of text, and each tool in the pipeline can transform that text in whatever way it deems appropriate. This makes it easy to extract data, sort it, and snip out the pieces you want to save.

A program's input normally comes from the keyboard, but can be redirected to come from a file instead – without having to change any of the programming code. Similarly, output normally is displayed on the screen, but can easily be redirected to a file instead, again without having to change any code. You can also send the program's output into a pipe, and it won't notice any difference. These capabilities are very powerful because traditional programming languages require you to write different code depending upon whether you want to send output to the screen, a file, a printer, or some method of interprocess communication like a pipe. Let's look at the basic symbols that Bash uses to denote these redirections.

Basic Bash I/O Redirection and Pipe Symbols	
< input_file_name	Take input from the designated file
> output_file_name	Send output to the designated file, overwriting any existing file of that name
>> output_file_name	Append output to the designated file; create it first if it doesn't exist
program1 | program2	Send the output of program1 as the input to program2

The above symbols work with stdin or stdout by default. We'll see that additional syntax is required if you want to deal with stderr as well, but let's start with some simple examples first.

For input redirection, we'll start with our familiar 'kitties.txt' file:

```
$ cat < kitties.txt
When the cat's away, the mice will play.
Two cats are better than one cat.
My youngest cat quickly becomes thoroughly
catatonic and listless after
eating a big bowl of catnip.

Cat is a GNU utility that is rarely used by
the cats in my neighborhood.
```

The 'less than' sign tells the 'cat' program to take its input from the file 'kitties.txt' rather than from standard input. In reality, this command produces the exact same results as you would get by typing

```
$ cat kitties.txt
```

So why bother with redirecting stdin? The answer is that you will almost never need to redirect standard input, at least in simple cases like this. Many of the command-line utilities that we have used can take a file or list of files as part of its input argument list. So you rarely need to redirect input at all. One classic example on UNIX systems was sending a predefined text file via the mail command:

```
$ mail < mail_message.txt
```

Modern mail programs don't really need this capability any more, since they can easily add attachments via the GUI. So for now, just be aware that redirecting input is possible, and don't worry about when you might need it.

Instead we will concentrate much more on redirecting *output,* since this is a capability that you will use all the time once you understand how it works. Let's also learn about a couple of additional GNU utilities that you might want to use in conjunction with redirection.

The two utilities are called 'head' and 'tail.' These commands show you the beginning lines of a file or the ending lines of a file, while ignoring everything in between. By default, each program shows ten lines of text, though you can use a '-number' option to specify how many lines you want to see. For example, if you wish to see the first five lines of 'kitties.txt,' you would type

```
$ head -5 kitties.txt
When the cat's away, the mice will play.
Two cats are better than one cat.
My youngest cat quickly becomes thoroughly
catatonic and listless after
eating a big bowl of catnip.
```

You can just as easily send this output to a file with the command

```
$ head -5 kitties.txt > first_five_lines_of_kitties.txt
```

The 'head' command reads its input from 'kitties.txt' and the 'greater than' sign causes standard output to be redirected to the file 'first_five_lines_of_kitties.txt.' Similarly, if you wanted to save the last two lines of 'kitties.txt,' you would type

```
$ tail -2 kitties.txt > last_two_lines_of_kitties.txt
```

You can verify that the command worked by typing

```
$ cat last_two_lines_of_kitties.txt
Cat is a GNU utility that is rarely used by
the cats in my neighborhood.
```

One important point to note about output redirection is that using '>' to create an output file **will overwrite any existing file of that name!** So be careful to only use output file names that don't already exist. We'll see in a later section that Bash provides a 'noclobber' option that prevents you from accidentally overwriting output files.

Now let's learn about pipes and the handy 'wc' (for 'word count') utility. The 'wc' command by default prints out the number of lines, number of words, and number of bytes for each file supplied in its argument list. For example,

```
$ wc kitties.txt
      8      46      260 kitties.txt
```

The command has additional options that allow you to select only one number for output. I usually use 'wc -l' to count only the number of lines in a file. However, through the magic of pipes, you can count other things as well. If I want to know the number of files in my home directory, all I need to do is type

```
$ ls | wc -l
     71
```

The strange character between the 'ls' and 'wc' commands is the vertical bar symbol, usually just above the <Enter> key on your keyboard (for American English keyboard layouts). In UNIX parlance, it is called a **pipe,** since the textual output from the 'ls' command is piped into the standard input of the 'wc' command. The 'wc' command then proceeds to count the number of lines that it received from stdin, in much the same fashion that it would if you had stored the output of 'ls' in a file. The result is almost the same as typing these two separate commands:

```
$ ls > ls.out
```

```
$ wc -l ls.out
     72 ls.out
```

There are a couple of minor differences. First, wc prints the name of the file in its output when it isn't reading input from stdin. Second, the number of lines is 72, because we just created a new file. The original command that used a pipe **did not create any output file.** Instead, the output of 'ls' was kept in memory and sent directly to the input of 'wc.' This is a form of **interprocess communication,** and is *much faster* than storing the output of 'ls' in a temporary file.

Sometimes you not only want a program's output to be stored in a file, you also want a record of any errors that occurred. This means that you not only want stdout redirected to a file, you want to make stderr go to the same file as well. As an example, we'll use the command that we used earlier to search for directories whose names begin with 'Program Files,' except this time we'll save all the output to a file:

```
$ find /c -name "Program Files*" -type d -print > find.out 2>&1
```

As in previous examples, the '> find.out' syntax says to store the standard output of the find command in a file named 'find.out' (in the current directory). The snippet at the end of the command ('2>&1) says to send stderr (the output from file descriptor 2) to the same place as stdout (the output from file descriptor 1); that is, send it to find.out.

Being able to easily save the output of a command to a file is great, but what do you do when you would like to *see* the output as it happens as well as save it to a file? That is easy to do with the GNU 'tee' command, which was designed for this purpose. Tee takes its input from a text stream; thus, **it must be used on the right-hand side of a pipe.** Tee writes the input stream to at least two different locations: the screen, and a list of one or more output files. The find command above could be written as

```
$ find /c -name "Program Files*" -type d -print | tee find.out
```

if you only want the standard output of find to be sent to the screen and saved to a file. If you want to redirect stderr as well, **you need to add the '2>&1' notation on the left-hand side of the pipe:**

```
$ find /c -name "Program Files*" -type d -print 2>&1 | tee find.out
```

This produces one output stream of text containing both stdout and stderr that goes into the input of the pipe. Then the tee command sends the output stream to both the screen and the output file. Note that, by default, tee overwrites its output file at the start of command execution, just like the '>' notation does. If you would rather append to the output file(s), use 'tee -a' instead. That is,

```
$ find /c -name "Program Files*" -type d -print 2>&1 | tee -a find.out
```

You aren't limited to using only one pipe. For example, how did I make up that list of 19 additional utilities included with Git that aren't .exe files? Here's how:

```
$ ls -F | egrep -v '(.exe|.dll)' | egrep '\*'
```

```
astextplain*
awk*
bunzip2*
c_rehash*
clear*
docx2txt*
echo*
egrep*
gitk*
gpg-zip*
gunzip*
printf*
pwd*
recodetree*
start*
vi*
vim*
which*
yacc*
```

First, I used the option to 'ls' that appends an asterisk to the names of executable files. Then I asked egrep to search for all executable files in the list that *don't* end in .exe or .dll (by using the '-v' option, which inverts the sense of the search). Finally, I search for those files remaining in the list that end with an asterisk to indicate that they are executable. (Note that the asterisk that egrep searches for needs to be escaped with a backslash; otherwise, the asterisk will be considered a regular expression character.) What if you just want to know how many such files there are? Simple, just add another pipe and use 'wc -l' to count the lines of output from ls after they have been filtered by the two calls to egrep:

```
$ ls -F | egrep -v '(.exe|.dll)' | egrep '\*' | wc -l
    19
```

Though in theory there is no real limit on the number of pipes in succession that you can use, in practice I recommend not going beyond three or four. The performance of your command can slow considerably once the number of pipes in use becomes more than a handful.

Bash Variables

As I mentioned near the start of the book, Bash is not just a command-line interpreter; it is in fact an entire programming language in its own right. And just like any other programming language, Bash can store values in **variables,** which are just human-readable names for memory locations. The syntax used is quite simple:

```
VARIABLE_NAME=value
```

Variable names can start with an underscore or letter, and can also contain numbers, as long as the variable doesn't start with a number. It is traditional to use uppercase variable names for shell variables, but it is not a requirement.

It is important to note that you can't put any spaces between the variable name and the equals sign, or between the equals sign and the value. You will get an error message if you do this.

The value that you store in a variable can be a text string or an integer. (Bash can't do calculations on floating-point numbers, though you could store a floating-point number as a string if you wish.) Here are some valid variable assignments:

```
$ DELAY=30
$ username=john
$ PROGRAM_FILES="/c/Program Files"
```

Note that if you assign a text string with spaces to a variable, the string must be enclosed in single or double quotes.

Predefined Variables and Positional Parameters

Bash has a large variety of predefined variables. Some of them are used to configure Bash, and others allow you to retrieve useful information. We will focus on the latter here. While there are a bunch of additional ordinary variables that are predefined, you'll notice that ones we discuss in this section are typically only one character long (not including the dollar sign). Here is a table of several of these variables; with the exception of $?, you won't use any of them very often:

Bash Predefined Single-Character Variables	
$?	Return status of last executed command
$-	List of options currently in effect
$$	Process number of the current Bash instance
$!	Process number of last background command
$_	Name of program at startup or value of last positional argument in last command.

$? will contain zero if the last command executed successfully, and a non-zero positive integer if the command *failed*. This may be counter-intuitive to people who don't come from a UNIX background. Zero represents *success*, and non-zero represents *failure* – exactly the opposite of what you might think!

There is another more interesting set of predefined variables, most (but not all) of which are single characters. These are referred to as **positional parameters**. Whenever a script is called with a set of arguments, all the appropriate positional parameters will be filled with values after Bash processes the line and breaks it up into chunks. Similarly, when a shell *function* is called with a set of arguments, it gets a set of positional parameters as well.

Bash Positional Parameters	
$#	Number of arguments, not counting command name
$0	Name of command, possibly including path
$FUNCNAME	Name of Bash function
$1-$9	First through ninth arguments
${n}	Braces are required for arguments with more than one digit
$* or $@	All arguments except $0
"$*"	All arguments except $0 returned as a single string
"$@"	All arguments except $0, with each argument individually quoted

The best way to understand the positional parameters is to look at some code and see the results. Try running the following script and observing the results. Then make changes to the arguments you supply and see what happens.

```bash
#!/bin/env bash

#       FILE:  argument_examples
#       ----------------
#
#       Demonstrate some of the different types of Bash command line
# arguments. Call this script with syntax like
#
# argument_examples junk whatever

#   Check how many arguments were supplied on the command line

echo
echo "The name of this script is:  $0"
echo

if [[ $# -gt 1 ]]
then
  echo "$# arguments were supplied to this script."
elif [[ $# -eq 1 ]]
then
  echo "$# argument was supplied to this script."
else
  echo "$# arguments were supplied to this script."
fi

echo "Positional parameter 1 is: $1"
echo "Positional parameter 2 is: $2"
echo "Positional parameter 3 is: $3"
echo
echo "The following set of arguments were supplied on the command
line:  $*"
echo "The following set of arguments were supplied on the command
line:  $@"
echo

#   Now let's try a shell function

function show_function_arguments ()
{
  echo "The name of this function is:  $FUNCNAME"
  echo
```

```
  #  Check how many arguments were supplied on the command line

  if [[ $# -gt 1 ]]
  then
    echo "$# arguments were supplied to this function."
  elif [[ $# -eq 1 ]]
  then
    echo "$# argument was supplied to this function."
  else
    echo "$# arguments were supplied to this function."
  fi

  #  List some of the arguments

  echo "Positional parameter 1 is: $1"
  echo "Positional parameter 2 is: $2"
  echo "Positional parameter 3 is: $3"
  echo
  echo "The following set of arguments were supplied on the command
line:  $*"
  echo "The following set of arguments were supplied on the command
line:  $@"
  echo
}

#  Call the function with different sets of arguments

show_function_arguments
show_function_arguments argument_one
show_function_arguments argument_one argument_two
```

An example run of the script is shown below:

```
$ argument_examples junk whatever

The name of this script is:  ./argument_examples

2 arguments were supplied to this script.
Positional parameter 1 is: junk
Positional parameter 2 is: whatever
Positional parameter 3 is:

The following set of arguments were supplied on the
```

command line: junk whatever

The following set of arguments were supplied on the
command line: junk whatever

The name of this function is: show_function_arguments

0 arguments were supplied to this function.
Positional parameter 1 is:
Positional parameter 2 is:
Positional parameter 3 is:

The following set of arguments were supplied on the
command line:
The following set of arguments were supplied on the
command line:

The name of this function is: show_function_arguments

1 argument was supplied to this function.
Positional parameter 1 is: argument_one
Positional parameter 2 is:
Positional parameter 3 is:

The following set of arguments were supplied on the
command line: argument_one
The following set of arguments were supplied on the
command line: argument_one

The name of this function is: show_function_arguments

2 arguments were supplied to this function.
Positional parameter 1 is: argument_one
Positional parameter 2 is: argument_two
Positional parameter 3 is:

The following set of arguments were supplied on the
command line: argument_one

argument_two
The following set of arguments were supplied on the
command line: argument_one
argument_two

The shift Builtin

The built-in 'shift' function is helpful when dealing with positional parameters. You
won't normally assign the value of $5 to a variable. Instead, a common idiom is to use
shift to move the positional parameters to the left; that is, the current value of $1
disappears, $2 becomes $1, $3 becomes $2, etc. Then everything can be done in terms
of $1. Here is an example program showing how this works:

```
#!/bin/env bash

#       FILE:   shift_example
#       -------------
#
#       Demonstrate the shift function. Call this script with syntax
like
#
# shift_example argument1 argument2 argument3

FIRST_ARGUMENT=$1
shift
SECOND_ARGUMENT=$1
shift
THIRD_ARGUMENT=$1

echo "This script was called with arguments ${FIRST_ARGUMENT},"
echo "${SECOND_ARGUMENT}, and ${THIRD_ARGUMENT}."

exit 0
```

If you run the program, you will see that is properly captures all the arguments that
were passed in:

```
$ shift_example argument1 argument2 argument3
This script was called with arguments argument1,
argument2, and argument3.
```

Prompt Variables

Bash has four prompt variables, $PS1, $PS2, $PS3, and $PS4. The primary prompt variable, $PS1, is the only one you are ever likely to care about. The primary prompt in Bash is a dollar sign, but you can easily change that value with an assignment like

```
$ export PS1='# '
#
```

or

```
# export PS1='Enter a Bash command: '
Enter a Bash command:
```

Save the new prompt definition in your .bashrc file (to be discussed soon) to make the change permanent. There are many fancy ways to display the prompt, including terminal commands to change the color. By default, Git Bash displays a two-line prompt, with the first line showing the user name, host name, and path to the current directory. The second line displays the standard dollar sign that we have been using in our examples. The default Git Bash prompt is actually quite complex:

```
$ echo $PS1
\[\033]0;$MSYSTEM:${PWD//[^[:ascii:]]/?}\007\]\n\
[\033[32m\]\u@\h \[\033[33m\]\w
$(__git_ps1)\[\033[0m\]\n$
```

It is a lot of fun to explore the many things that you can display with the prompt, but this is a subject well beyond the scope of this book. For a nice discussion of some of the possibilities, with examples and useful tables, try this site:

https://wiki.archlinux.org/index.php/Color_Bash_Prompt

As an example, I modified the second line of my prompt to display the history number, day of week, and date/time (all in boldface yellow) with the following setting in my .bashrc file:

```
export PS1="\[\033]0;$MSYSTEM:${PWD//
[^[:ascii:]]/?}\007\]\n\[\033[32m\]\u@\h\[\033[33m\]\w$
(__git_ps1)\[\033[0m\]\n\[$BYellow\][H:!] \d \@ $ \
```

```
[$Color_Off\]"
```

Make sure that the value for $PS1 is really one line of code. Now that we've had a bit of fun, it is time to learn about the difference between local and global variables.

Local Versus Global Variables

The variables that we have seen so far are considered **local variables.** They are local to the current instance of the Bash shell. But it is also possible to start a new instance of Bash from the command line; this is known as a **subprocess** or **subshell.** It is a brand-new process that can run independently of the parent shell. All of Bash's external commands are run as subprocesses as well. What if some of those commands need access to a variable that was defined in the parent shell? This is where global variables come in handy. A **global variable** or **environment variable** will have its value exported to all subprocesses of the shell where it was defined. The syntax for creating a global variable requires one extra step:

```
GIT_VERSION_NUMBER="1.9.0"
export GIT_VERSION_NUMBER
```

The 'export' command makes the value of the variable available to all subprocesses. Thus, if you wanted to run an external program that uses a feature unique to the latest version of Git, you could check the Git version number to make sure you are using the latest version. You can also export variable names in only one line, just like we did with the $PS1 prompt variable in the previous section:

```
export GIT_VERSION_NUMBER="1.9.0"
```

Once you have assigned a value to a variable, how do you access it? Just put a dollar sign in front of it. For example, if we create local variables like

```
$ OLD_FILE=oldfile
$ NEW_FILE=newfile
```

Then we could rename 'oldfile' to 'newfile' with a command like

```
$ mv $OLD_FILE $NEW_FILE
```

Things get a bit trickier if the value in the variable contains spaces. In that case, the variable needs to be enclosed in double quotes. We could create a variable that holds a directory name and then cd to that directory with commands like

```
$ PROGRAM_FILES='/c/Program Files'

$ cd "$PROGRAM_FILES"
```

Look carefully at the two lines above. Even though the value that we assigned to $PROGRAM_FILES was already enclosed in (single) quotation marks, we have to surround the variable name *again* with double quotation marks when we reference it in the 'cd' command. This is true regardless of whether we used single or double quotes in the variable assignment. This is because Bash replaces the name of the variable with its value, and if that value contains spaces, Bash will try to examine each piece of the variable's value as a separate argument. Enclosing the value in double quotes still allows the variable's value to replace the variable name, but keeps it from being broken up by the shell. This is an issue because Bash does the variable replacements before it breaks up the command line into individual words.

Double quotes have a special meaning when one or more variable names are inside the quotation marks. They cause Bash to do what is often called **variable interpolation.** That is, it substitutes the value of the variable for the variable name itself. You can use this capability to assign values to variables where the value itself contains another variable. For example, if you need to look at the directory containing Internet Explorer on a regular basis, you could do something like the following:

```
$ IE_DIRECTORY="${PROGRAM_FILES}/Internet Explorer"

cd "$IE_DIRECTORY"
```

The double quotes in the variable assignment cause the whole path to Internet Explorer to be stored in $IE_DIRECTORY, and since that path contains spaces, we need to put double quotes around it again for use in the cd command. Note that if you only use single quotes, Bash will treat the variable name as a literal string and you'll get an error like

```
$ cd '$IE_DIRECTORY'
sh.exe": cd: $IE_DIRECTORY: No such file or directory
```

On the other hand, if you leave out the quotation marks entirely, Bash will try to change to a directory named '/c/Program' because it broke up the path name into a space-separated list of arguments to cd:

```
$ cd $IE_DIRECTORY
sh.exe": cd: /c/Program: No such file or directory
```

Note that when we assigned a value to $IE_DIRECTORY above, we referenced $PROGRAM_FILES as '${PROGRAM_FILES}.' Including the curly braces around the variable name in addition to the dollar sign at the front is the most politically correct way to refer to variables in Bash. The braces ensure that Bash can always figure out where the end of the variable name is, even if it is directly followed by other text. It is good practice to include the curly braces, but it isn't necessary as long as there is no ambiguity about where the end of the variable is.

You can remove global or local variables with one command, for example:

```
$ unset IE_DIRECTORY
```

Don't put a dollar sign in front of the variable name, or you will get error messages. (You only prepend the dollar sign [and possibly add curly braces] when you *use* a variable; not when you set its value, export it, or delete it.)

Using env and set to Look at Global and Local Variables

The external 'env' command is used to display a list of all global or environment variables and their values. If you type the command without any options, you'll see that the list of variables is not in alphabetical order. This is a case where I/O redirection comes to the rescue. To get a nicely ordered list, we can simply pipe the output of env into the 'sort' utility (use 'sort -r' to sort in reverse order):

```
$ env | sort
!::=::\
ALLUSERSPROFILE=C:\ProgramData
APPDATA=E:\Users\Michael Hanna\AppData\Roaming
COMMONPROGRAMFILES(X86)=C:\Program Files (x86)\Common
Files
COMMONPROGRAMFILES=C:\Program Files (x86)\Common Files
COMMONPROGRAMW6432=C:\Program Files\Common Files
```

.
.
.

You'll see a long but ordered list of all your environment variables. What if you want to look at local variables?

That isn't so easy. You need to use the 'set' builtin command to do this. Typing

```
$ set
```

will display *all* of your shell variables, both global and local. In addition, it will display any shell functions that are defined, *along with their source code.* This is probably not what you want. You can easily extract only the variable definitions by piping the output of set into egrep:

```
$ set | egrep '^\w+='
ALLUSERSPROFILE='C:\ProgramData'
APACHE=/c/xampp/apache
APACHE_BIN=/c/xampp/apache/bin
APPDATA='E:\Users\Michael Hanna\AppData\Roaming'
BASH=/bin/sh
BASH_ARGC=()
BASH_ARGV=()
BASH_LINENO=()
BASH_SOURCE=()
BASH_VERSINFO=([0]="3" [1]="1" [2]="0" [3]="1"
[4]="release" [5]="i686-pc-msys")
BASH_VERSION='3.1.0(1)-release'
COLUMNS=80
```
.
.
.

The regular expression that we used to filter the output of set can be expressed in English as "look for at least one word character at the beginning of a line, followed by an equals sign" (with no intervening spaces). This gives you a list of both local and global variables, while ignoring the functions entirely. If you wanted to extract the local variables only, you would have to jump through more hoops, such as writing a script in Python or Ruby. (This essentially involves computing the difference between two sets, a capability that is not built into Bash. Bash would have to use arrays and a double loop to do this kind of task. Bash is not always the best tool for the job.)

On occasion you might only be interested in knowing what functions are defined. You can extract the function names with a command like

```
$ set | egrep '^\w+[[:space:]]+\(\)'
__git_aliased_command ()
__git_aliases ()
__git_commands ()
__git_complete ()
__git_complete_file ()
```

In this case, the regular expression can be translated as "look for at least one word character at the beginning of a line, followed by at least one space character, followed by a pair of parentheses" (with no space between them). You need to put backslashes in front of the parentheses to prevent them from being interpreted as regular expression metacharacters.

Using set and shopt to Set and Unset Shell Options

Not only does Bash use lots of predefined variables to govern its configuration, there are also *two different sets* of configuration options which are *not* stored in Bash variables. Worse yet, the 'set' command controls the setting and unsetting of one set of these options. This is *very* confusing. To see the options that can be configured by the set builtin (and the current values of the options), type

```
$ set -o
allexport       on
braceexpand     on
emacs           off
errexit         off
errtrace        off
functrace       off
hashall         on
histexpand      on
history         on
ignoreeof       off
```

```
interactive-comments    on
keyword          off
monitor          on
noclobber        off
noexec           off
noglob           off
nolog            off
notify           off
nounset          off
onecmd           off
physical         off
pipefail         off
posix            off
privileged       off
verbose          off
vi               on
xtrace           off
```

We mentioned the 'noclobber' option earlier, which will prevent Bash from overwriting existing files when you do I/O redirection. We can see above that this option is off by default. Turn it on by typing

```
$ set -o noclobber
```

If you type the 'set -o' command again (without any additional arguments), you should see that this option is now on. To prove that it works correctly, create a temporary file and then try to write to it via I/O redirection:

```
$ touch junk.txt
```

```
$ ls > junk.txt
sh.exe": junk.txt: cannot overwrite existing file
```

You can turn the option off again by typing

```
$ set +o noclobber
```

If you try the I/O redirection again,

```
$ ls > junk.txt
```

you'll see that junk.txt has been silently overwritten, and now contains your directory listing.

Note that the syntax for setting and unsetting options is bass-ackwards from what it should be: You use 'set -o option_name' to *set* an option, and 'set +o option_name' to *unset* an option. This is the kind of thing that makes new Linux users gnash their teeth in frustration. But there are more complexities as well.

There is a second set of internal Bash options controlled by the 'shopt' builtin. Just type the command to see the value of all the current settings:

```
$ shopt
cdable_vars          off
cdspell              off
checkhash            off
checkwinsize         off
cmdhist              on
dotglob              off
execfail             off
expand_aliases       on
extdebug             off
extglob              off
extquote             on
failglob             off
force_fignore        on
gnu_errfmt           off
histappend           off
histreedit           off
histverify           off
hostcomplete         on
huponexit            off
interactive_comments      on
lithist              off
login_shell          on
mailwarn             off
no_empty_cmd_completion off
nocaseglob           off
nocasematch          off
nullglob             off
```

```
progcomp          on
promptvars        on
restricted_shell          off
shift_verbose     off
sourcepath        on
xpg_echo          off
```

You'll note that there is some overlap with the options controlled by set. You can set options with shopt with a command like

```
$ shopt -s nullglob
```

You can unset the option with

```
$ shopt -u nullglob
```

To add to the confusion, you can also use shopt to set and unset options that are normally controlled by set! To do this, use syntax like

```
$ shopt -o -s noclobber
```

Unset the variable with the command

```
$ shopt -o -u noclobber
```

Confused yet? I certainly am! The good news is that you will probably only choose to change a small handful of options, if any. And you can store the values that you decide to set in your .bashrc file for permanent use. Once you have done this, you can forget about everything you read here until the next rare occasion that you might want to change one of these values.

The Power of Aliases

Variables store a value, but **a Bash alias is shorthand for an action.** For example, I always set a common alias for the 'ls' command:

```
$ alias ll='ls -l'
```

When I type 'll,' the 'ls -l' command is executed. This only saves a small amount of typing, but the savings can add up fast when you define aliases for actions that you constantly do.. Another one I like is to define

```
$ alias up='cd ..'
```

This is less awkward than typing the periods to move up to the parent directory. I can also clear the screen with the DOS-like command

```
$ alias cls='clear'
```

which is ironic because the provided 'clear' command is really calling cmd.exe to execute the 'CLS' command!

If you want to easily list your shell functions, you can avoid retyping the somewhat complex filter we used earlier by creating an alias like this:

```
alias list_shell_functions="set | egrep '^\w+[[:space:]]+\(\)'"
```

If you decide to learn the Git version control software, you'll find that some of its commands can be rather lengthy too. For example, to find out what files were modified in the most recent commit, I can use an alias like

```
$ alias lgit="git log -1 --name-status | egrep '^[ACDMRTUXB]'"
```

As you can see above, aliases can include multiple commands separated by pipes or redirection characters, as well as arguments to each of the commands.

Aliases are also convenient for moving to commonly-used directories with long path names. For example, if you take online classes on Coursera or some similar platform, you might define an alias like

```
alias bio_boot_camp='cd "${EDUCATION}/Coursera
Classes/MathematicalBiostatisticsBootCamp"'
```

(which should be entered all on one line). Typing 'bio_boot_camp' is a lot easier than typing out the whole directory path. Or, if you are really lazy, you could use 'bbc' as the alias.

The Power of Shell Functions

One deficiency of aliases is that they can't take arguments when you type them on the command line. For example, once you have defined the 'lgit' alias in the previous section, you cannot use a command like

```
$ lgit *.php
```

to check for the most recently modified PHP files. (It wouldn't make any sense to do this anyway, since the file names would have to be given to the 'git log' command, not to the output that we selected from that command.)

Bash functions work much like the functions in many other programming languages. The function takes an action and returns a value of 0 if it succeeded, or some non-zero value if it didn't. It can also take arguments. One example that I use all the time is

```
function sw() { cd "../${1}" ; }
```

Bash functions can take arguments from $0 to $9, or greater. $0 is the name of the program or function itself; the rest of the arguments can be used to pass information into the function. For the simple function above, I just want to make it easy to switch to a sibling directory; i.e. one that is at the same level in the directory hierarchy.

Suppose that we have a parent directory named 'food' and two subdirectories, 'fruits' and 'vegetables.' If I am currently in 'food/fruits,' I can switch to 'food/vegetables' by typing 'sw vegetables.' (I use 'sw' as an abbreviation for 'switch.')

Subshells

A subshell can be started by typing

```
$ bash
```

This starts a new instance of Bash, which will inherit the environment variables that were defined in the parent shell. When you are done with the subshell, leave by typing

```
$ exit
```

If you want to temporarily start a subshell from within the current instance of Bash, use this syntax:

```
$ (command1; command2; … )
```

All the commands inside the parentheses will be run in the subshell as soon as you hit <Enter>, and then you will be returned to the prompt of the shell you started from. You can use I/O redirection to save the result to a file, or even send the output into a pipe. For example, suppose you are currently in 'food/fruits' and you want to look at the contents of 'food/vegetables' without actually moving to that directory. One way to do this is to type

```
$ ls -l ../vegetables/*
-rw-r--r--    1 Michael  Administ         0 Mar 21 15:14 ../vegetables/durian
-rw-r--r--    1 Michael  Administ         0 Mar 21 15:14 ../vegetables/kiwi
-rw-r--r--    1 Michael  Administ         0 Mar 21 15:14
../vegetables/pineapple

../vegetables/rutabaga:
total 0
```

Using a subshell, you could instead type

```
$ (cd ../vegetables; ls -l)
total 0
-rw-r--r--    1 Michael  Administ         0 Mar 21 15:14 durian
-rw-r--r--    1 Michael  Administ         0 Mar 21 15:14 kiwi
-rw-r--r--    1 Michael  Administ         0 Mar 21 15:14 pineapple
drwxr-xr-x    2 Michael  Administ         0 Mar  1 16:28 rutabaga
```

The two commands produce somewhat different output. In the first case, the path you specified is prepended to the file name. Also, directory listings are handled slightly differently. Suppose that we are still in the 'fruits' directory but we want to save the contents of the 'vegetables' directory in our current location for convenience. You can do this easily with a subshell:

```
$ (cd ../vegetables; ls -l) > vegetables.txt

$ cat vegetables.txt
total 0
-rw-r--r--    1 Michael  Administ         0 Mar 21 15:14 durian
-rw-r--r--    1 Michael  Administ         0 Mar 21 15:14 kiwi
```

```
-rw-r--r--     1 Michael   Administ         0 Mar 21 15:14 pineapple
drwxr-xr-x     2 Michael   Administ         0 Mar  1 16:28 rutabaga
```

Note that if you had put the redirection inside the parentheses, then the file would
have been saved to the *subshell's* current directory; namely, 'vegetables:'

```
$ (cd ../vegetables; ls -l > vegetables.txt)
```

```
$ cat ../vegetables/vegetables.txt
total 0
-rw-r--r--     1 Michael   Administ         0 Mar 21 15:14 durian
-rw-r--r--     1 Michael   Administ         0 Mar 21 15:14 kiwi
-rw-r--r--     1 Michael   Administ         0 Mar 21 15:14 pineapple
drwxr-xr-x     2 Michael   Administ         0 Mar  1 16:28 rutabaga
-rw-r--r--     1 Michael   Administ         0 Mar 21 15:21 vegetables.txt
```

This time, the output file is included in the directory listing, since it stored in the same
directory where the 'ls' command was being done (and '>' creates the output file
before the 'ls' command is executed.)

Other Shells

On UNIX and Linux systems, there are a variety of shells available, and you can start
any of them at any time. On Windows, you can also invoke other shells. For example,
if you need to do a few quick DOS commands, there is no need to fire up a separate
DOS window. Instead, just type

```
$ cmd.exe
Microsoft Windows [Version 6.1.7600]
Copyright (c) 2009 Microsoft Corporation. All rights
reserved.

C:\Program Files (x86)\Git\bin>
```

Voila! You are in the same directory that you were in Bash, and you can now type in
DOS-style commands. Type 'exit' to leave. If you would rather run Windows
PowerShell, type

```
$ powershell.exe
Windows PowerShell
```

```
PS C:\Program Files (x86)\Git\bin>
```

Again, type 'exit' to leave. If you are a real glutton for punishment, you can even
invoke PowerShell from cmd.exe! While I only use DOS commands about once a
year on average, it's nice to know that I don't have to go hunting through the menus to
start a DOS box.

Command Substitution

I mentioned previously that Bash's external commands also run in a subshell. One
variation on this theme is called **command substitution.** You can run a command and
store the output in a shell variable. A simple example uses the external 'date'
command to store a string representing the current date:

```
$ DATE=$(date)
```

```
$ echo $DATE
Thu Mar 13 01:29:14 PDT 2014
```

Note that command substitution uses the syntax

```
$ $(command)
```

where the first dollar sign is simply the Bash prompt (if you aren't using it in a script).
The other dollar sign in front of the opening parenthesis is required. On the other
hand,

```
$ (command)
```

where the dollar sign is again the Bash prompt, starts the command in a subshell.

The 'date' command has many options, so you can choose almost any date format you
want. For example,

```
$ DATE=$(date +%Y-%m-%e)
```

```
$ echo $DATE
2014-03-13
```

Simply provide the options to the command inside the parentheses just as you would at the command line. Command substitutions are even nestable. Note that these commands only operate on stdout by default. You have to add '2>&1' to the end of the command (inside the parentheses) if you also want the standard error output. (In this particular example, you may be confused by the fact that the 'date' command uses a plus sign to start its formatting argument. This is a non-standard notation for command-line arguments, but the 'date' command has used this notation for a long time.)

I'll note for completeness that there is also an older syntax for command substitution: Simply enclose the command in grave accents (sometimes called 'backticks'). The grave accent is usually to the left of the '1' key (in the upper left corner) on modern American keyboards. For example,

```
$ DATE=`date`
```

This syntax is not nearly as flexible and is no longer recommended.

Configuring Bash with the .bashrc File

We have learned about a few of the ways to configure Bash, we know how to store data in variables, we know how to create aliases, and we've even seen a simple example of a shell function. These capabilities are all very useful, but if you type them in at the command line like we have been doing, they will be lost whenever you exit your Bash window. Instead, it is better to collect all the variables, aliases and functions that you want to use regularly and save them in a **.bashrc** file. Bash looks for a file of this name every time a new instance of Bash starts up, and runs the commands in the file. So you only have to define all these things once.

Where is the .bashrc File?

The file is located in your home directory. Since the file name begins with a period, it is considered a 'hidden' file that is not normally displayed, but if you type

```
$ ls .bashrc
.bashrc
```

you should see it. If you don't have a copy of this file, open your favorite text editor and create it. We'll show some examples of the types of commands you might want to put into the .bashrc file. Note that you can use '#" to denote the start of a comment; all Bash comments extend to the end of the line.

Editing and Sourcing the .bashrc File

After you make changes to the .bashrc file, they won't have any effect on your currently open Bash windows. You need to re-execute the .bashrc file by running the 'source' command in each open Bash window. 'Source' is another Bash builtin, and there are actually two ways to invoke it:

```
$ source ~/.bashrc
```

or

```
$ . ~/.bashrc
```

Yes, a period is a synonym for the 'source' command! And the tilde is Bash shorthand for your home directory.

The Critical Importance of Setting the Proper $PATH Variable

$PATH is an environment variable used by Bash. It contains a list of directory names (separated by colons). Whenever Bash is trying to execute a command that is not built into Bash, it has to know where to find it. What it does is to search each of the directories in $PATH in succession until it finds the desired external command. Then it executes the command and shows the results. What if there are two commands of the same name in different directories? Bash will execute whichever one it finds first. For example, your Git installation includes the Perl programming language, version 5.8.8 (a relatively old but very stable release). On the other hand, the XAMPP development environment (a popular package for doing PHP Web development) also includes its own version of Perl; in my case, version 5.16.3. If you want to use the more recent version of Perl, you'll need to ensure that the directory for the XAMPP software is listed earlier in the path than the directory for Git's utilities.

Windows also has its own PATH variable, and Bash's $PATH inherits some values from it. But Bash's $PATH variable is independent of that of Windows and is stored separately. You can add your own directories to Bash's $PATH without affecting your Windows PATH environment settings.

What I normally do is to store each directory path in a Bash variable, and then concatenate all the variables into one long string, with each variable separated by a colon and the whole mess surrounded by double quote marks. My $PATH variable in its full glory looks like this:

```
PATH="${DEFAULT_PATH}:${VIM}:${XAMPP_PERL_BIN}:$
{GOW_BIN}:${PIK_BIN}:${RUBY_BIN}:${HEROKU_BIN}:${PHP}:$
{PYTHON_BIN}:${SQLITE}:${XAMPP}:${APACHE_BIN}:$
{R_LANGUAGE_BIN}:${OCTAVE_BIN}:${MYSQL_BIN}:$
{VIRTUALBOX}:${FILEZILLA}:${NOTEPAD_PLUS_PLUS}:$
{SUBLIME_TEXT_2}:${OTHER_BIN}"
export PATH
```

This is pretty ugly, but not as bad as typing out the full path for each variable in $PATH. Notice that I have a variable called $DEFAULT_PATH as part of my path. This variable holds the default value of $PATH before any .bashrc file has been created; i.e., the value that is inherited from the Windows PATH variable. The "normal" way to add elements to the path is to use syntax like

```
PATH="${PATH}:${SOME_OTHER_DIRECTORY}"
```

This is the syntax used for later examples in the book, but it has one disadvantage: Every time you re-invoke the .bashrc file (also known as re-sourcing it), your $PATH variable will keep growing longer and longer (because it always adds material to the existing $PATH value), which can sometimes lead to weird errors. If you want to avoid this issue, run the command

```
$ echo $PATH
```

before you create your .bashrc file. Then store the output value in a variable called $DEFAULT_PATH or whatever name you want, and add all new path elements after that (separated by colons).

We'll see more examples of how to add directories to $PATH when we start discussing how to use some of your favorite programs with Git Bash.

Storing Variables, Aliases and Shell Functions in .bashrc

Here is a (relatively simple) .bashrc file that shows how to store all your configuration information in one place:

```
#        FILE:   .bashrc
#                -------
#
#        Defaults for the Git Bash shell. Remember to source
# this file in each open Bash window after you change it!

#-----------------------------------------------------------------------------
#  Define some common directory names
#-----------------------------------------------------------------------------

PROGRAM_FILES='/c/Program Files'
PROGRAM_FILES_X86='/c/Program Files (X86)'

DEFAULT_PATH=".:/bin:/c/windows/system32:/c/windows:/c/windows/System32/Wbem:/c/windo
ws/System32/WindowsPowerShell/v1.0/:/c/Program Files (x86)/MiKTeX
2.9/miktex/bin/:/c/Program Files (x86)/Heroku/bin:/usr/cmd"

#  Note that any variables referenced in your $PATH need to be defined
#  earlier in your .bashrc file.

PATH="${DEFAULT_PATH}:${VIM}:${XAMPP_PERL_BIN}:${GOW_BIN}:${PIK_BIN}:${RUBY_BIN}:$
{HEROKU_BIN}:${PHP}:${PYTHON}:${SQLITE}:${XAMPP}:${APACHE_BIN}:${R_LANGUAGE_BIN}:$
{OCTAVE_BIN}:${MYSQL_BIN}:${VIRTUALBOX}:${FILEZILLA}"
export PATH

#-----------------------------------------------------------------------------
#  Define convenient aliases for switching to local directories
#-----------------------------------------------------------------------------

alias home="cd $HOME" #  Was git_home
alias app_data='cd "${HOME}/Application Data"'
alias downloads='cd "${HOME}/Downloads"'
alias my_documents='cd "${HOME}/Documents"'
alias my_music='cd "${HOME}/Music"'
alias my_videos='cd "${HOME}/Videos"'
alias program_files='cd "/c/Program Files"'
alias program_files_x86='cd "/c/Program Files (x86)"'

#-----------------------------------------------------------------------------
#  General aliases
#-----------------------------------------------------------------------------

alias cls='clear'
alias dir='ls -p'
```

```
alias cdir='ls -a -F --color'
alias ll='ls -l'
alias up='cd ..'
alias sb='source "${HOME}/.bashrc"'
alias no_beep='net stop beep'  #  Turn off error bell in MySQL and Vim
alias swapd='pushd +1'

#--------------------------------------------------------------------------
#  Set Bash configuration variables
#--------------------------------------------------------------------------

set -o vi          #  Do line editing in vi mode
set -o noclobber   #  Don't allow I/O redirection to destroy files

#--------------------------------------------------------------------------
#  Shell functions
#--------------------------------------------------------------------------

#  Switch to a sibling directory with syntax like 'sw directory_name'

function sw() { cd "../${1}" ; }
```

In later sections, we'll need to add to the $PATH definition to tell Bash where to find your favorite editor and other tools. Add these definitions to your existing $PATH variable; don't create a new $PATH variable each time. Otherwise, only the final definition of $PATH will be used.

More Advanced Bash

Now we'll discuss some of the elements of Bash that are used for writing shell scripts. These capabilities go beyond the types of things you would normally put in your .bashrc file. By putting Bash commands into a separate executable shell script, you make them available for use in the same fashion as any other UNIX or Linux tool.

The Bash Programming Language

As I mentioned previously, Bash is not only a command-line interpreter, it actually supports a fairly complete programming language. It does not include every feature of modern programming languages like Java, Ruby, or Python. There are no objects, functions are fairly limited, and you can't do computations on floating-point numbers. Only one-dimensional arrays are supported (and I don't plan to cover them here, since they aren't that frequently used). On the other hand, there is a large variety of built-in tests, if statements, case statements, and for, while, and until loops. And these structures provide some capabilities that you won't see in other languages, such as the ability to apply I/O redirection to the input and output of loops.

I will only give a brief introduction to most of these features, since the primary emphasis of this book is to teach you how to configure Bash to make it easy to work with the many included utilities.

Writing Scripts

Bash scripts can be saved in a file with any name; no special extension is required, though some people like to use a '.sh' extension. One important thing to know is that after you save your file, you want to change its permissions to make it executable (if it isn't already). We'll do this with the 'chmod' or change mode command. If you have a Bash script named 'do_something,' you can make it executable by typing

```
$ chmod +x do_something
```

This allows you to run the script by typing

```
$ do_something
```

```
I did something.
```

If the script weren't explicitly made executable, you would have to run it with a command like

```
$ bash do_something
I did something.
```

The contents of the file are fairly simple:

```
#! /bin/env bash

#       FILE:   do_something
#               ------------

echo "I did something."

exit 0
```

Comments start with a pound sign ('#') or hash mark, and extend to the end of the line. The first line is special; it is commonly referred to as the 'shebang line.' The shebang is the symbol '#!' followed by a command denoting what program should be used to run the script. It used to be common to invoke a shell directly with syntax like

```
#!/bin/sh
```

but it is better practice now to pass the name of the program to run to the env command instead. Our script really contains only one actual command that produces output; namely, the 'echo' command. The 'exit 0' command is optional (since Bash will do this when it reaches the end of the file anyway), and exits the program. The return status of '0' is considered a successful outcome, while a non-zero return status denotes an error. You can follow the above template for all of the Bash scripts that you write. (We will only show code snippets for most of the examples, but remember that a complete Bash script must start with a shebang line.)

If-Then-Else Statements

Let's start our exploration of if statements by examining a simple but complete script:

```
#!/bin/env bash

#       FILE:  days
#              ----
#
#       Experiment with days of the week.

echo -n "Enter the name of a day:  "

read DAY_NAME

if [[ "$DAY_NAME" = 'Monday' ]]
then
   echo "I don't like Mondays."
fi
```

There are several new things in the above script. First, note that the echo command uses the '-n' option, which prevents it from ending the line. The read command (which is also a shell builtin) reads a value typed in by the user and stores it in the variable $DAY_NAME. We used 'echo -n' so that the user could type in the answer on the same line as the prompt.

Next, we see the if statement. The **condition** for the test is enclosed inside a double set of square brackets. Bash also supports tests using two older and equivalent forms:

```
if [ condition ]
then
   statement
fi
```

or

```
if test condition
then
   statement
fi
```

The double brackets have more capabilities and are preferred in modern Bash scripts.

We are doing a string comparison, so we use a single equals sign to compare the contents of the variable on the left to the quoted string on the right. It is good practice to always put the variable name inside of double quotes, just in case there are spaces inside it. Spaces will cause Bash to get confused when it tries to read the condition inside the brackets.

If you want the 'then' clause to be on the same line as if, you have to add a semicolon:

```
if [[ condition ]]; then
  statement
fi
```

This is actually a general rule for running multiple commands on one line. Each command must be separated by a semicolon, and the commands will be run in succession from left to right. For example,

```
$ pwd; ls
```

Also pay attention to the condition inside the square brackets of an if statement. There must be a space between the opening brackets and the beginning of the condition, and another space after the end of the condition and before the closing brackets. Omit the spaces and you will get syntax errors. This is more restrictive than a lot of other languages.

When you run the days script, you should see example output like this:

```
$ days
Enter the name of a day:  Monday
I don't like Mondays.
```

It is easy to add another test to our code by including an 'else' statement:

```
if [[ "$DAY_NAME" = 'Monday' ]]
then
  echo "I don't like Mondays."
else
  echo "But other days are okay."
fi
```

We get the alternate output if we *don't* enter 'Monday' when we run the program:

```
$ days
Enter the name of a day:   Wednesday
But other days are okay.
```

It is good to note that our bare-bones program does no error checking to verify that a valid day of the week was entered:

```
$ days
Enter the name of a day:   Zeepsday
But other days are okay.
```

We can additional conditions with the 'elif' statement. (Note the spelling carefully. Most other programming languages use the syntax 'elsif' or 'else if.')

```
if [[ "$DAY_NAME" = 'Monday' ]]
then
  echo "I don't like Mondays."
elif [[ "$DAY_NAME" = 'Tuesday' ]]
then
  echo "It must be Belgium."
else
  echo "But other days are okay."
fi
```

Case Statements

We can write very similar code using a case statement instead.

```
case "$DAY_NAME" in
  Monday)   echo "I don't like Mondays."
            ;;
  Tuesday)  echo "It must be Belgium."
            ;;
  *)        echo "But other days are okay."
            ;;
esac
```

'*)' is the default case if no previous value matches $DAY_NAME. Note that an if statement ends with 'fi' (the reverse of 'if') and a case statement ends with 'esac' (the reverse of 'case'). Many other languages would use an 'end' or 'end if' statement instead. Is it better to use if or case statements? Case statements are not strictly necessary, and are considered by some language designers to be 'syntactic sugar.' However, if you need to test a lot of different cases (all the days of the week for example), a case statement can be easier to read and maintain. Note, however, that the response to each case must be followed by two semicolons at the end of the line or on a separate line.

Testing Conditions

There are many types of tests that can be used in the condition for an if statement. (Some of these tests are also useful in testing the conditions for loops.) You cannot use these tests in a case statement. The tests can be divided into three major categories: Numeric tests, string tests, and file tests. You can also do multiple tests, AND and OR operations, and negate tests. There are some additional tests which are less frequently used, and some tests that are not applicable to a Windows environment. We'll only list some of the most common tests here:

Grouping and Negation for Tests	
(expression)	Group compound expressions; true if whole expression is true
! expression	True if expression is false
expression1 && expression2	True if expression1 *and* expression2 are true
expression1 || expression2	True if expression1 *or* expression2 are true

Note that the AND and OR tests use what is known as 'short-circuit evaluation.' This means that if the truth of the whole expression can be determined by only looking at the first element, the second element will never be evaluated.

Numeric Comparisons	
expression1 -eq expression2	True if the two expressions are numerically equal
expression1 -ne expression2	True if the two expressions are *not* numerically equal
expression1 -lt expression2	True if expression1 is less than expression2
expression1 -gt expression2	True if expression1 is greater than expression2
expression1 -le expression2	True if expression1 is less than or equal to expression2
expression1 -ge expression2	True if expression1 is greater than or equal to expression2

String Comparisons	
string	True if string is not null
-n string	True if string has non-zero length
string = pattern or string == pattern	True if string matches pattern
string != pattern	True if string does *not* match pattern
string1 \< string2	True if string1 comes lexicographically before string2
string1 \> string2	True if string1 comes lexicographically after string2

Note that because '<' and '>' are also used for I/O redirection, they must be escaped with a backslash character when used for string comparisons to prevent Bash from getting confused and doing the wrong thing.

Next are some of the most common file comparison tests.

File Comparison Tests	
-d file	True if file is a directory
-e file	True if file exists
-f file	True if file is a regular file
-r file	True if file is readable
-s file	True if file has non-zero size (implies existence)
-w file	True if file is writable
-x file	True if file is executable
-z file	True if file has zero length

For Loops

For loops in Bash actually have a variety of forms, some of which are markedly different from those of other programming languages. We'll start with a commonly used idiom, which has the loop iterate through a list of elements:

```
for element in list
do
   commands
done
```

Suppose that each time you create a new version of your software, you want to use a make file to build the new release for your development, qa, and production versions. (A **make file** is a set of instructions on how to build a software system by compiling multiple files and possibly installing the software in a separate location. Note that the make utility is *not* included with Git, but it is included with another set of tools that we'll discuss later, called the "GNU on Windows" utilities.) A separate make file will be in each directory, possibly with different instructions for each type of build. We could build three new versions of the software with a for loop like this:

```
for DIRECTORY in development qa production
do
   #  Make sure the directory really exists before cd-ing
```

```
to it.

   if [[ -d $DIRECTORY ]]
   then
     cd $DIRECTORY
     echo "Starting software build in directory
$DIRECTORY"
     make
     cd ..
   fi
done
```

The for loop provides a space-separated list of three directory names, one of which is assigned to the variable $DIRECTORY each time through the loop. We test to make sure the directory really exists just in case of typos in the code. Note that we don't need to put double quotes around $DIRECTORY in the if statement or in the cd command since there are no spaces in the directory names. But it would be a good idea to include the quotation marks anyway in case you decide to add such a directory name to the list in the future. In that case, you would also need to quote the directory name in the list, since the for statement breaks up its input list based on spaces. For example, if we changed the 'qa' directory to 'quality assurance,' you would need code like

```
for DIRECTORY in development "quality assurance"
production
do
   #  Make sure the directory really exists before cd-ing
to it.

   if [[ -d "$DIRECTORY" ]]
   then
     cd "$DIRECTORY"
     echo "Starting software build in directory
$DIRECTORY"
     make
     cd ..
   fi
done
```

In both examples we did a cd to multiple directories. Remember that after you cd to each subdirectory, you'll normally want to go back to the parent directory with the 'cd ..' command.

Bash for loops can also use shell file globbing to create a list of files to process. For example,

```
for FILE in "*.pdf"
do
  echo "Found file $FILE"
done
```

However, this code won't work properly if there are no .pdf files in your directory. In this case the file globbing expression expands to itself. That is, the file variable is set to hold the literal value "*.pdf." You'll get output like

```
Found file *.pdf
```

which is not correct. There two ways around this problem. One way is to define the 'nullglob' Bash option. Add the following line to your code (before the loop):

```
shopt -s nullglob
```

This causes the file glob to return a null string if nothing matches the expression. This will prevent the loop from being executed at all. Another alternative is to make sure that the file actually exists before you try to do anything with it:

```
for FILE in *.pdf
do
  if [[ -e "$FILE" ]]
  then
    echo "Found file $FILE"
  fi
done
```

This is slightly less efficient in that the loop will still be executed once even if no matching files are found.

Another thing that you can do with a for loop is to explicitly store the list of files you want to iterate through in a variable:

```
FILES_TO_ARCHIVE="./document1.txt
./letter3.txt
./new contract12.txt"

for TXT_FILE in $FILES_TO_ARCHIVE
do
  #  If the file exists, process it

  if [[ -e "$TXT_FILE" ]]
  then
    #  Strip off the extension
    FILE_STEM=$(basename "$TXT_FILE" .txt)

    #  Create a backup
    echo "Creating backup file ${FILE_STEM}.bak"
    cp "$TXT_FILE" "${FILE_STEM}.bak"
  else
    echo "Error:  File $TXT_FILE is missing."
    exit 1
  fi
done
```

When you store a list of files in a variable, you must be careful to put each file on a separate line and then enclose the whole list in quotes. However, even if you follow this advice, the above example won't work. The problem is that our list of files has a file name with a space in it. Bash and many of the GNU utilities often don't handle file names with embedded spaces well by default. This is because Bash wants to break up text into words separated by spaces. The good news is that we can change this behavior by using the $IFS (Internal Field Separator) variable. By setting this variable to a new value (and then resetting it afterward if we want the default behavior again), we can make the example code work even for file names with spaces. Add code like this before the for loop

```
IFS_original=$IFS

IFS=$(echo -en "\n\b")
```

and then add the line

```
IFS=$IFS_original
```

after the loop is complete. Note that when the example code processes each file, it uses the external 'basename' command to strip the '.txt' extension off the end of each file name we're interested in. There are other ways to accomplish the same result, but this is one of the traditional ways to do it.

If you prefer C-style for loops controlled by a numeric counter, you can do this in Bash too, but you need to enclose the loop condition inside a *double* pair of parentheses:

```
UPPER_BOUND=10

for ((i=0; i < UPPER_BOUND; i++))
do
   echo "Loop $i"
done
```

The first part of the loop condition initializes the value of $i; the second part is the actual condition that is tested each time through the loop, and the third part (i++) increments the value if $i at the end of each iteration. Notice that you don't need the dollar sign to refer to $i inside the double parentheses.

You can even do an infinite loop in a manner similar to a C for loop:

```
for ((;;))
do
   echo "Infinite loop - getting tired yet?"
done
```

Interrupt the program by typing <Ctrl-c>; otherwise, like the Energizer bunny, it will just keep going, and going, and going.

Break and Continue Statements

Any loop can have break or continue statements. The break statement is the most commonly used, and its purpose is to break out of a loop before it has finished executing. If you provide a numeric argument like 'break 2,' it will break out of multiple nested loops instead of just one.

Continue is rather like the opposite of break, but not quite. Rather than quitting the loop prematurely, the continue statement says to *stop* the current iteration of the loop, go back to the top, and immediately *start* the next iteration of the loop.

Let's look at a somewhat contrived example that implements a simple menu system. It has nested while loops and multiple case statements. The inner while loops use 'break 2' or 'continue 2' to break out of or continue the outer while loop, while the outer while loop only needs to use break or continue. One unfamiliar bit of syntax may be the form of the loop:

```
while :
```

The colon is Bash-speak for a null statement. It is the equivalent of saying 'while true;' that is, it starts an infinite loop. You *must* use a break statement to get out of an infinite loop. The only other choice is to type <Ctrl-c> at the command line. The code is shown below. Experiment by adding some menu choices of your own.

```
#  Break and continue example

while :
do
   echo      "Menu"
   echo      "----"
   echo
   echo      "eat"
   echo      "drink"
   echo
   echo -n "Enter a choice (exit to end):   "

   read choice

   case "$choice" in
     eat)
       while :
       do
     echo -n "Burger or fries? (exit to end):   "

     read food
```

```
    case "$food" in
      burger)
        echo "Mmm, burned cow flesh!"
        echo
        continue 2
        ;;
      fries)
        echo "Yummy oil-soaked starch!"
        echo
        continue 2
        ;;
      exit)
        break 2
        ;;
      *)
        echo "Error:  Unknown option"
        echo
        continue
        ;;
    esac
    done
    ;;
drink)
  while :
  do
echo -n "Coke or Pepsi? (exit to end):   "

  read drink

  case "$drink" in
    Coke)
      echo "Mmm, high-fructose corn syrup!"
      echo
      continue 2
      ;;
    Pepsi)
      echo "Mmm, high-fructose corn syrup!"
      echo "(Can you tell any difference)?"
      echo
```

```
            continue 2
            ;;
        exit)
            break 2
            ;;
        *)
            echo "Error:   Unknown option"
            echo
            continue
            ;;
      esac
    done
    ;;
  exit)
    break
    ;;
  *)
    echo "Error:   Unknown option"
    echo
    continue
    ;;
  esac
done
```

While Loops

Except for the last example in the previous section, for loops are normally executed a fixed number of times. While and until loops can be executed any number of times, depending on the condition that controls the loop. While loops have their condition evaluated at the top of the loop. If the condition is FALSE the first time through, the loop will never be executed at all. The general form of a while loop is

```
while [[ condition ]]
do
   statements
done
```

(You can put the condition inside a single pair of square brackets if you prefer.) For example, you can easily create a loop controlled by a counter with code like

```
UPPER_BOUND=10
i=0

while [[ $i -lt $UPPER_BOUND ]]
do
  echo "Loop $i"
  let i=i+1
done
```

You'll notice that we have a let statement at the bottom of the loop, which allows us to increment the counter. You don't need to use the dollar sign at the front to reference variables like $i inside the let statement. If the let statement is not present, you will get a weird error when Bash tries to process the assignment statement to increment the value of $i:

```
Loop 0
./while_loop_examples: line 11: [[: i+1: expression
recursion level exceeded (error token is "i+1")
```

While loops are often used in scripts that allow multiple command line arguments, just like any other UNIX or Linux tool. Let's try to create our own tool and allow it to accept a few arguments. We'll improve our previous example for creating backup files. We'll start by processing command-line options with a while loop and a case statement. Once we know what options the user has selected, we'll use a for loop to actually create the backup files. We'll also do some error checking to avoid obvious problems with what the user typed. Finally, we assume that the script will operate on all files specified in the current directory. (A nice exercise for the reader is to see if you can make it apply to all subdirectories of the current directory as well.) This is a more complex script than any that have been shown so far, so I'll list it in its entirety below:

```
#!/bin/env bash

#      FILE:  create_backups
#             --------------
#
#      Back up the specified files in the current directory using options
# provided by the user.

#  Usage message and help text
```

```
USAGE="Usage: create_backups [-h | --help | -v | --version \
--source-ext=dot-plus-3-character-extension]"

#  Default extension of files to back up

SOURCE_EXT=".txt"

#  Version number of this tool

VERSION="Version 1.0"

#----------------------------------------------------------------------
#  Process command-line arguments
#----------------------------------------------------------------------

while [[ "$1" ]]
do
  case "$1" in
    -h | --help)
      echo "$USAGE"
      exit 0
      ;;

    --source-ext=\.[a-z][a-z][a-z])
      #  Assign text to the right of the equals sign to $SOURCE_EXT
      SOURCE_EXT="${1#--source-ext=}"
      shift
      ;;

    -v | --version)
      echo "$0 $VERSION"
      exit 0
      ;;

    --)
      #  End of all options
      shift
      break
      ;;

    -*)
      #  Unknown short or long option
      echo "Error:  Unrecognized option $1" >&2
      echo "$USAGE"
      exit 1
      ;;

    *)
      #  Unknown text on command line
      echo "Error:  Unknown text $1" >&2
      echo "$USAGE"
      exit 1
      ;;
  esac

done

echo "Source extension is ${SOURCE_EXT}"
```

```
#  Use date format 2014-03-31-10-58-06

DATE=$(date +%Y-%m-%e-%H-%M-%S)

#-----------------------------------------------------------------------------
#  Process all matching files in current directory
#-----------------------------------------------------------------------------

for FILE in $(echo "./*${SOURCE_EXT}")
do
  #  If file is non-zero in size, process it

  if [[ -s "$FILE" ]]
  then
    #  Strip off the extension
    FILE_STEM=$(basename "$FILE" "$SOURCE_EXT")

    #  Create the backup file name
    BACKUP_FILE="${FILE_STEM}${DATE}.bak"

    echo "cp $FILE ${BACKUP_FILE}"

    #  Do the copy or issue an error if it didn't succeed

    cp "$FILE" "${BACKUP_FILE}" || \
    echo "Error:  Failed to create file ${BACKUP_FILE}."

  fi
done

echo "All done."

exit 0
```

I tried out the script in a directory that contained files like the following:

```
$ ls
blob1.dll   create_backups   fancy file.txt   grab_bag.txt   wherever
blob2.dll   crud.pdf         file.txt         whatever       whomever
```

Note that the file 'fancy file.txt' has a space embedded in it. This added some complexity to the script. When the script is run using the default extension of '.txt' for the source files, you should see results like

```
$ create_backups
Source extension is .txt
cp ./fancy file.txt fancy file2014-03-31-15-46-10.bak
cp ./file.txt file2014-03-31-15-46-10.bak
cp ./grab_bag.txt grab_bag2014-03-31-15-46-10.bak
All done.
```

If you use an alternate extension for the source files, you'll see a different result:

```
$ create_backups --source-ext='.dll'
Source extension is .dll
cp ./blob1.dll blob12014-03-31-15-47-19.bak
cp ./blob2.dll blob22014-03-31-15-47-19.bak
All done.
```

You can also try the other options:

```
$ create_backups --version
./create_backups Version 1.0
```

If you give an invalid option, you'll get an error message:

```
$ create_backups --last-week
Error:  Unrecognized option --last-week
Usage: create_backups [-h | --help | -v | --version
--source-ext=dot-plus-3-char
acter-extension]
```

Sorry, you can't go into the past and create the backups after you already deleted the original files!

Now let's examine how the script works. We assume that all files we want to back up have a three-character extension, '.txt' by default. We also assume that we want our output file to have the '.bak' extension.

We use a while loop and a case statement to process the arguments supplied on the command line. If you look carefully at the code, you'll notice that the argument processing is flawed; it doesn't really allow use of multiple arguments or combinations of arguments. For example, 'create_backups -vh' won't work. Taking care of possibilities like this is what makes production scripts so complex. Since our goal here is mainly to illustrate the concepts, we won't worry about every last detail. It makes conceptual sense to only deal with one argument at a time in this script anyway.

The most complex part of the argument processing is checking to see whether the user wishes to specify a different file extension for the files to back up. This uses some syntax we haven't seen up to now:

```
--source-ext=\.[a-z][a-z][a-z])
    # Assign text to the right of the equals sign to
$SOURCE_EXT
    SOURCE_EXT="${1#--source-ext=}"
    shift
    ;;
```

First, the case statement uses a regular expression that matches an argument of the form '--source-ext' followed by a period, followed by three lowercase alphabetic characters. Once we have the argument we want, we then need to strip off the characters to the left of the extension and assign only the period and three lowercase letters to the $SOURCE_EXT variable. We get rid of the characters by using what is known as **parameter substitution.**

This uses a special syntax of the form

```
${variable_name|special characters|pattern}
```

to operate on variable_name . (The pipe characters above are just visual separators, not part of the syntax.) In our case, we are taking the value of positional parameter $1 as the variable name to operate on. The special character is '#,' which tells Bash to strip out the pattern (in this case, '--source-ext=') from the left end of $1's value. We then take that new value and store it in $SOURCE_EXT.

There are actually something on the order of 25 different types of operations you can perform using parameter substitution, and this a subject that tends to confuse beginners, so we aren't going to do anything more with it here.

Once we know what source file extension we want to use, we will next use a for loop to process all the files in the current directory that match that extension. The common solution for doing this would be something like

```
for FILE in *.txt
do
  commands
done
```

but we have two extra problems to consider: We want to handle file names that include spaces, and we want to retrieve the desired extension from a variable. This requires more complex syntax:

```
for FILE in $(echo "./*${SOURCE_EXT}")
```

Here we are actually using command substitution with '$()' to take the output of the echo command as the list of files for the for loop. The echo command uses a file glob to get the list of files in the current directory, and since the file names may contain spaces and the file extension is stored in a variable, we must enclose the whole argument to echo in double quotes.

Next, we remove the file extension using the basename function. For example, 'my_document.txt' would become 'my_document.'

```
#  Strip off the extension
FILE_STEM=$(basename "$FILE" "$SOURCE_EXT")
```

Now we can append the date and the .bak extension to the stem of the file name:

```
#  Create the backup file name
BACKUP_FILE="${FILE_STEM}${DATE}.bak"
```

You can experiment with the date command to find a date/time format that you like. Just be aware that Windows won't like it if you use colons to separate hours:minutes:seconds values, so don't use that form for your backup file name. (I used hyphens in my date format.)

Finally, the cp command copies the original file name to the name of the backup file.

```
#  Do the copy and issue an error if it didn't succeed

cp "$FILE" "${BACKUP_FILE}" || \
echo "Error:  Failed to create file ${BACKUP_FILE}."
```

There are several things to notice about the copy command. First, the command is continued onto a second line of the script by putting a backslash character right before the end of the line. This tells Bash that the two lines are really one command. We also use the double pipe symbol '||' to indicate an OR operation of the form

```
command1 || command2
```

If command1 succeeds, the second command will not be executed. If command1 fails, command2 *will* be executed. You can see the error message in action if you change your date format to use colons to separate the hours:minutes:seconds values. (You'll also get an error message from the cp command itself.)

Redirecting I/O for Loops

One interesting capability of Bash loops that you won't find in most other programming languages is that you can perform I/O redirection *on an entire loop*. One nice example that you'll occasionally see discussed online is how to look at files when your system has run out of memory. System administrators will want to reboot a system that has run out of memory, but first they might want to look at the contents of the file that they believe caused the problem. If the system is out of memory, you can't run external commands like cat or less, but Bash's built-in commands are already loaded into memory. By typing in a whole loop at the command line, you can look at the contents of a file. First, we'll do it by typing in the loop components one line at a time. After the first line, Bash is smart enough to know you are entering a loop, and gives you the secondary prompt '>' to ask for the rest of the loop:

```
$ while read line
> do
>   echo "$line"
> done < addresses.txt
Wherever
P.O. Box 993771
Durham, NC. 02331

Somewhere
334 Twit Terrace
Camden, NJ 32976-2813

Elsewhere
403 Road Kill Lane
Austin, TX. 84703
```

You can also do this command as a one-liner by separating the pieces of the loop with semicolons:

```
$ while read line; do echo "$line"; done < addresses.txt
Wherever
P.O. Box 993771
Durham, NC. 02331

Somewhere
334 Twit Terrace
Camden, NJ 32976-2813

Elsewhere
403 Road Kill Lane
Austin, TX. 84703
```

Until Loops

In most programming languages, the condition for a while loop is tested at the top of the loop, which means the loop may never get executed at all. An until loop typically gets tested at the bottom of the loop, which means that an until loop will always be executed at least once. Bash unfortunately does not follow this paradigm.

Instead, Bash until loops work like while loops; both test the condition at the top of the loop. You can prove this with a code snippet like this

```
until [[ 1 -eq 1 ]]
do
  echo "Did loop at least once."
done
```

The loop produces no output, so the echo statement inside the loop was never executed even once. Because Bash's until loops don't behave as people would expect from other languages, I don't see much point in using them. You can get the same results with a while loop.

Using Your Favorite Editor from Git Bash

The single most indispensable tool for a programmer is a **text editor.** At least for the purpose of this book, I am going to assert that the term 'text editor' has a very specific meaning that is different from a word processor. A text editor's primary function is to edit plain text; it can add text, delete text, or change it in a variety of ways. A programmer's text editor is not concerned with using multiple fonts or type styles; it doesn't care about formatting paragraphs, tables, or lists. This is because programming language compilers don't care about these niceties. They simply care about what keywords and other information are present in the text, and the order in which that text appears. This is enough information to allow the compiler to translate a human-readable programming language into the low-level instructions that your hardware understands.

A **word processor,** on the other hand, is primarily useful for *formatting* text. Programs with a modern graphical user interface like Microsoft Word make it easy to change type fonts and apply numerous styles to your text, such as boldface, italics, underlining, or strikethrough. You can format paragraphs with drop caps or hanging indents, you can create tables with borders or numbered lists in a variety of formats. If you are writing a book, you can even generate tables of contents and indices. There is a price for all of this power, however. All of the text in your Word document has to be stored with hidden formatting codes that tell your word processor how to treat the different pieces of text. If you write a computer program in Word and ask your compiler to compile and run your program, your compiler will likely have an onset of severe stomach cramps and proceed to projectile vomit a large mass of error messages. This is because compilers don't know about the formatting codes used by word processors and regard them as alien intruders that disrupt the meaning of the program. So you should never use a word processor to write a computer program.

Word processors have one additional problem: Most of them are surprisingly poor at *editing* text! To a large degree, this problem is due to the unnecessary obsession with mouse-based editing. (pioneered by Xerox PARC and later used by both Apple and Microsoft). Mouse-based editing is great if you are cutting and pasting anywhere from a few words to a few screen pages of text. But it doesn't work very well at all when you consider the more pathological cases that crop up in real-world text editing. For example, if you need to change the first character of every line of your document, you will find this an incredibly tedious process if you try to do it with a mouse. At the other extreme, if you are writing a 500 page book, what happens when you need to move the 40 pages of Chapter 12 to Chapter 14? Odds are that after a loooong scroll with the mouse, you'll overshoot the intended end of your selection and have to scroll backward. In the process of scrolling back and forth, you will almost certainly lose your selection and have to start over again.

The better programmer's editors solved these types of problems long ago, and many other issues that are of particular concern for writing code. For example, most computer code should be indented for readability, and some programming languages (notably Python) *require* specific types of indenting, so most programmer's editors provide an autoindent option. Programmer's text editors also can provide language-specific syntax coloring and extremely sophisticated search-and-replace operations.

Regardless of which text editor you prefer to use, it is not difficult to configure Bash to invoke that editor from the command line. (You can still invoke an editor from the Startup menu or by double-clicking on its icon if you like, but there are some advantages to starting your editor from the command line. For example, when you start an editor from the command line, your current working directory will be where the editor saves your file by default. This is what you usually want. If you just double-click on the editor's icon, you'll often have to use the "Save As..." dialog to pick another location to save your file.)

Vim and GVim

Two of the original UNIX editors, vi and emacs, are still popular today decades after they were invented. Though vi (short for 'visual editor' and pronounced 'vee eye') is still directly used on some systems, many Linux distributions have replaced it with Vim. Vim is a vi clone whose name means 'Vi iMproved.' Not only is Vim freely available for multiple platforms (though the author Bram Moolenaar asks for donations to his favorite charity in Uganda), it provides numerous additional features that go far beyond the original capabilities of vi. The GUI version of Vim, called 'gVim,' allows you to use multiple windows (and tabs within windows). It also provides mouse support, though experienced users won't feel much need to touch the mouse. You will find vi or Vim on every UNIX or Linux system that I am aware of, so it is well worth learning at least the rudiments of how they work.

You can use the non-graphical version of Vim directly from Bash, since it is provided with Git. Just type

```
$ vim file_name
```

(Note that the actual command is in lowercase letters. Type ':q' to quit, or ':wq' to write the file and quit.) The gVim program provides a graphical user interface and menus that help make Vim a little more user-friendly for Windows users. It also allows multiple files to be displayed as tabs in a single window, and provides icons for easy cutting and pasting. GVim is not provided by Git, so you will have to install it separately. Fortunately, you can get a Windows installer for it at

```
http://www.vim.org/
```

On the 'Download' page, choose the 'gvim74.exe' installer, which is the most current release at this writing. If a newer version is available, use it. Double-click on the installer to start the installation. The first screen you will see is

Click 'Yes' to continue the installation. After you see the license agreement,

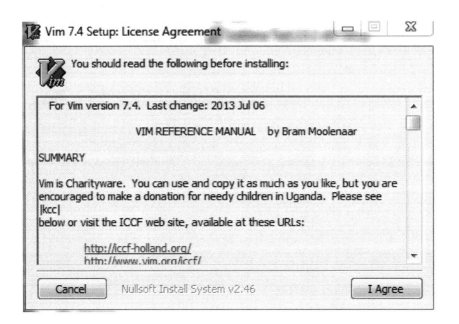

click 'I Agree' (even if you don't; otherwise, the installation will terminate). Next, you will see the installation options.

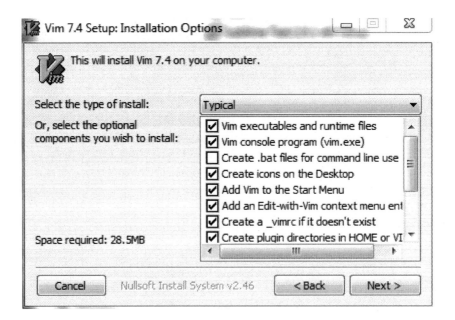

I recommend accepting the default options and clicking 'Next.' You will now have an opportunity to choose the folder into which Vim should be installed.

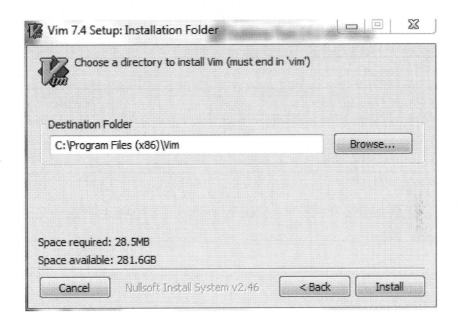

Unless you have a specific reason to put it elsewhere, I again recommend accepting the default path and then clicking 'Install.' You'll see that the installation requires 28.5 MB of space, which is a lot more than the original vi (which could fit on a floppy), but much less than many contemporary editors that don't have nearly as many features. After the installation is done, you'll see a notice that it is complete.

When you click 'Close,' you'll see a final message asking if you want to read the release notes. It is always a good idea to check them, but you don't have to.

After the installation is done, you will find three gVim icons on your desktop. Double-click any of the icons to start gVim. I normally use the 'gVim 7.4' icon, but there are two others that you may find helpful. If you want to open a critical file on a read-only basis (to prevent accidental changes to the text), then you'll want to double-click on the 'gVim 7.4 Read only' icon. If you are used to a modeless editor where you can start typing as soon as the editor comes up, you may prefer the 'gVim 7.4 Easy' icon, which starts gVim in text insertion mode.

You can start any of these versions of gVim from the Bash command line. You just need to add the directory containing the gVim executables to Bash's $PATH variable. Do this by adding lines like the following to your .bashrc file:

```
VIM="${PROGRAM_FILES_X86}/Vim/vim74"

PATH="${PATH}:${VIM}"
export PATH
```

This appends the Vim directory to the existing list of directories that Bash will search to find gvim. If your $PATH definition already contains references to multiple directories, you can add the Vim directory anywhere in the path, as long as you have no other version of gVim on your system:

```
PATH="${PATH}:${VIM}:${RUBY_BIN}:${PHP}:${PYTHON}:$
{XAMPP}:${APACHE_BIN}:${MYSQL_BIN}:${VIRTUALBOX}"
export PATH
```

(You should have only one definition of the $PATH variable, and each directory path in your definition should be separated from the preceding one by a colon character. If you have more than one definition of a variable in your .bashrc file, the last definition will take precedence, and earlier versions will be ignored.) After you save the changes to your .bashrc file, you now need to source that file in each open Bash window by typing

```
$ source ~/.bashrc
```

Alternatively, you could use the 'sb' alias that I previously suggested adding to your .bashrc file. To test that Bash can properly find gVim, you can type the command

```
$ gvim --version
```

You will see a large amount of information about the options that your copy of gVim was compiled with. Then you can open files by typing

```
$ gvim file_name &
```

(I recommend starting gVim as a background process; that way, you can continue to use your Bash window while the gVim window is running. This lets you easily switch back and forth between using the gVim window for editing and saving, and then using the Bash window to run your program.)

If Bash can't find the right directory that holds the gvim executable (note that the executable name is spelled with lowercase letters), you'll get an error message like

```
$ gvim
sh.exe": gvim: command not found
```

If you see this error, check your $PATH definition carefully and be sure that a colon separates each element of the $PATH list. Be sure to note that you will need to re-source the .bashrc file each time you change the $PATH definition.

You can start gVim in 'Read only' mode from Bash by using the command

```
$ gvim -R file_name &
```

You can also start gVim in 'Easy' mode with the command

```
$ gvim -y file_name &
```

To learn more about using gVim in 'Easy' mode, type

```
:help Easy
```

or

```
:help evim-keys
```

Note that the supposedly 'Easy' version of gVim keeps you in Insert mode most of the time, which is completely contrary to the original intent of both vi and Vim. In all other forms of Vim, you can use what Vim calls 'normal mode' (and what Vi calls 'command mode') by hitting the <Esc> key. That won't work in 'Easy' mode. Instead, you have to use the more difficult key sequence of typing <Ctrl-L> (lowercase 'l' works too). I don't recommend using gVim in this mode unless you are completely clueless about how Vim works. Anyone with even a modicum of experience in vi or Vim will quickly grow frustrated enough to give up in disgust.

Assuming that you can now get access to gVim, here is an example of something you can do from the command line that you can't do with a mouse:

```
$ gvim -p *.c &
```

This command will open every C program file in the current directory *in a separate tab* (or pane) in one gVim window! Vim and gVim have many other handy startup options that you can explore on your own.

Vim is hands-down the most powerful text editor that I have ever used. While it does have a steep learning curve, anyone who aspires to be a professional programmer should learn it, as vi or Vim may be the only editor available on some systems. Keep in mind that you don't have to learn every command to be an effective user of Vim. You'll find it easier to learn in small doses.

It is also important to note that vi and Vim are the only editors I have ever used that are reasonably well designed for touch typists. You can perform the vast majority of editing operations while keeping your hands centered on the 'home row' keys. Virtually all other editors require extensive use of the Control or Alt keys (and/or the mouse), which is not conducive to easy typing. Any programmer who is a touch typist (and any programmer who claims to be a professional *should* be a touch typist) will find that putting some effort into learning Vim will pay off with years of increased productivity.

Emacs

Emacs is the other most famous editor from the early days of UNIX. Emacs has so many features and modules that it could be thought of as an entire IDE. Indeed, someone once said something to the effect that "Emacs is a great operating system; too bad it doesn't come with a decent text editor."

Emacs is not available in the form of a Windows installer program; instead, you will have to download a compressed .zip file and unpack it in a directory of your choice. Recent versions of emacs are available here

```
http://ftp.gnu.org/pub/gnu/emacs/windows/
```

As of this writing, the most recent file that you will wish to download is emacs-24.3-bin-i386.zip, which is ~47 MB in size. (You'll see that it expands to a hefty 163 MB after you unpack it.) Before downloading the file, create a directory to put it in:

```
$ cd /c
```

```
$ mkdir emacs

$ cd emacs
```

(You could just as easily put the emacs directory in '/c/Program Files' if you prefer.)
Now download the .zip file and make sure it is present in the emacs directory:

```
$ ls -l
total 23875
-rw-r--r--    1 Michael  Administ 48894234 May 23 15:11
emacs-24.3-bin-i386.zip
```

We'll use the GNU 'unzip' utility to extract the files from the .zip archive:

```
$ unzip emacs-24.3-bin-i386.zip
```

You'll see a huge list of files being unpacked, which may take a minute or two. After
the lava flow of bits has stopped invading your hard drive, you'll see that the emacs
directory still contains the original .zip file and a new directory:

```
$ ls -F
emacs-24.3/  emacs-24.3-bin-i386.zip
```

To save space, you can delete the .zip file:

```
$ rm emacs*.zip
```

Let's take a quick peek at the contents of the new emacs subdirectory:

```
$ ls -F emacs-24.3
BUGS  COPYING  README  README.W32  bin/  etc/  info/
leim/  lisp/  site-lisp/
```

In UNIX parlance, the /bin directory is where executable files are stored. We want to
know the location of the executable that actually runs the editor.

```
$ cd emacs-24.3/bin
```

```
$ ls -F
```

```
COPYING          ctags.exe*        emacs.exe*           etags.exe*     movemail.exe*
addpm.exe*       ddeclient.exe*    emacsclient.exe*     hexl.exe*      profile.exe*
cmdproxy.exe*    ebrowse.exe*      emacsclientw.exe*    libXpm.dll*    runemacs.exe*
```

Now you have two choices for how to run emacs in the background (so that you can still use the Bash window that you started from):

```
$ runemacs
```

or

```
$ emacs &
[1] 5776
```

Strangely, if you invoke the editor by using runemacs, it doesn't show up in Bash's process list. When the editor starts, you'll see a friendly window like the following:

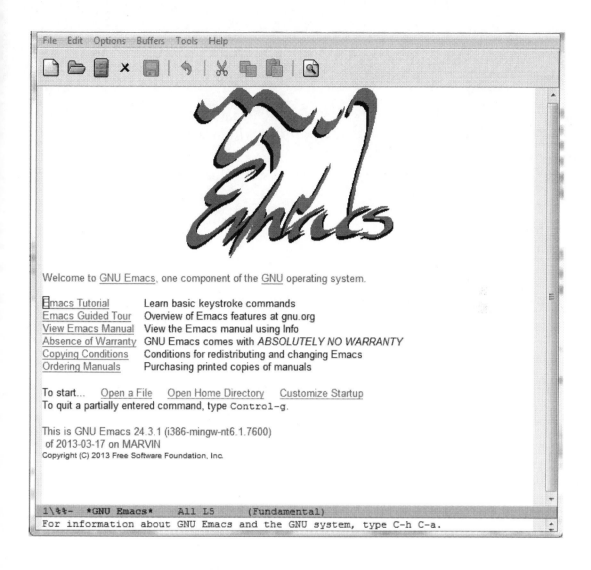

Note that you cannot exit from the program with the traditional Windows <Alt-F4> command. Instead, you can click on the Close box, choose 'File->Quit' from the menu, or use the traditional emacs command <Ctrl-x><Ctrl-c>. (To save your work, you can use <Ctrl-x><Ctrl-w> or choose 'File->Save As...' from the menu.)

We have proven that we can invoke emacs from the directory containing the editor itself, but if we want to make it available from any directory in Bash, we must once again add some code to our .bashrc file.

```
EMACS="/c/emacs/emacs-24.3/bin"
```

```
PATH="${PATH}:${EMACS}"
export PATH
```

Source the .bashrc file in each open window or alternatively, close each Bash window and re-open it. Now you can open files with emacs from any directory. For example, you can now use emacs to edit your .bashrc file if you wish:

```
$ cd
```

```
$ emacs .bashrc &
[2] 5244
```

If you want some additional (Windows-oriented) help on installing and configuring emacs, you can try these links:

```
http://tahirhassan.blogspot.com/2011/08/installing-emacs-
on-windows-7.html
```

```
http://www.claremontmckenna.edu/pages/faculty/alee/emacs/
emacs.html
```

Notepad++

If you are new to programming, learning Vim or emacs may seem like even more effort than learning your first programming language. Many beginners on Windows systems try to write programs using Notepad. Notepad may be fine for writing very small files, but the problem is that Notepad has almost no actual editing features, so it is completely unsuitable for making extensive changes or working on large programs.

A popular alternative to Notepad that provides a reasonable number of the editing capabilities that programmers typically need is Notepad++. You can get the program by going to

```
http://notepad-plus-plus.org/
```

and clicking the 'download' link. For convenience, download the Notepad++ Installer package. Double-click on the file to start the install. You'll see a dialog asking you to select your preferred language (human language, that is, not programming language):

After making your choice, click 'OK' to continue. Now you will see the Setup screen.

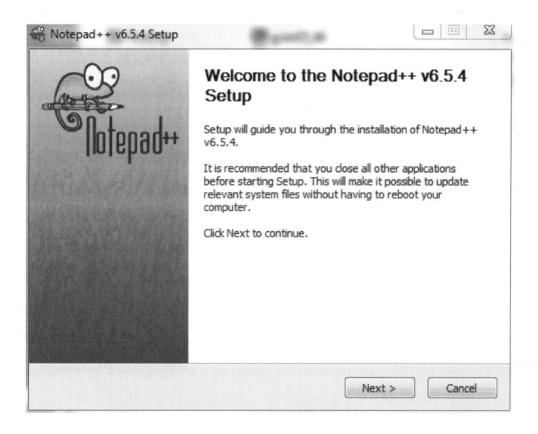

Just click 'Next' to go to the next screen. Now you will see the Notepad++ license agreement:

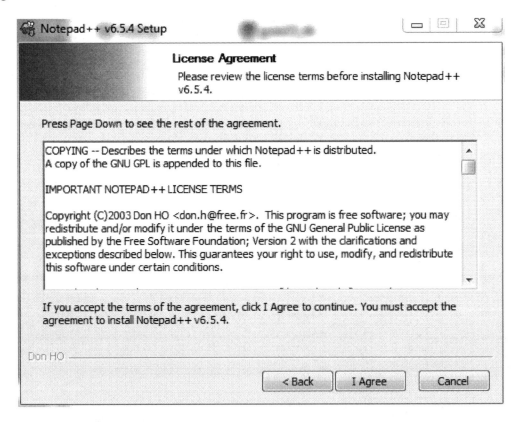

Click 'I Agree' to continue. Next, you get an opportunity to change the default installation location.

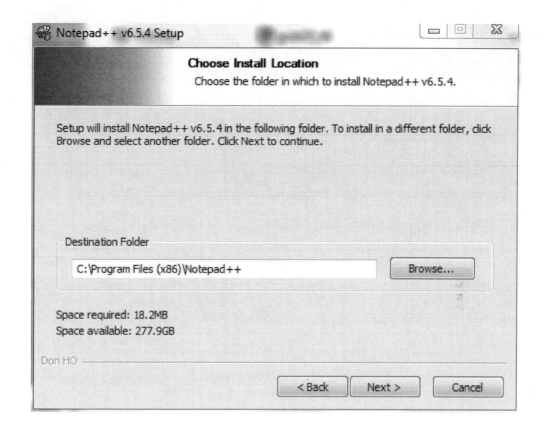

I recommend accepting the default and clicking 'Next' to continue. Now you get to choose which components of the software you wish to install:

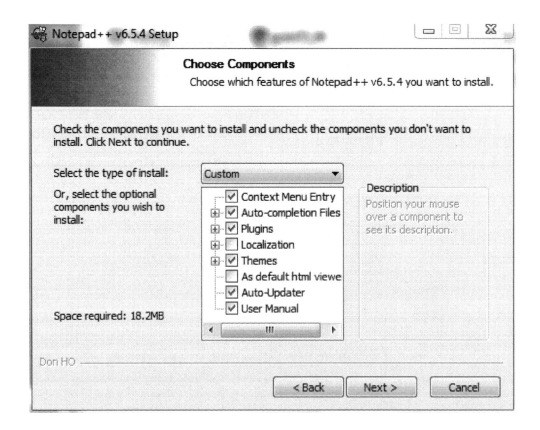

I recommend accepting the default choice of components and clicking 'Next' to continue. You'll get a final set of options before the installation begins:

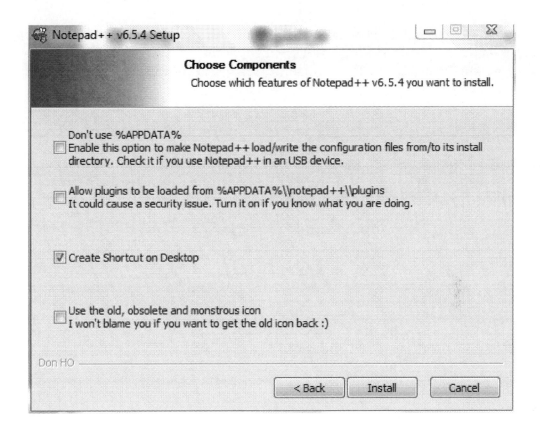

I recommend allowing the installer to create a shortcut for Notepad++ on your desktop. If you intend to run Notepad++ from a USB drive, check the first check box as well. Then click 'Install' to start the installation. You'll see a final dialog telling you that the installation was successful.

If you leave the check box to run Notepad++ checked, then when you click Finish, Notepad++ will start up and give you an editing window. You can also double-click on the desktop shortcut to activate the editor, or add it to your Start menu. You can also run it directly from Bash if you don't want to bother with the mouse.

Just like we did with Vim, you will need to add a couple of lines to your .bashrc file:

```
NOTEPAD_PLUS_PLUS="/c/Program Files (x86)/Notepad++"

PATH="${PATH}:${NOTEPAD_PLUS_PLUS}"
export PATH
```

Note that the plus sign can't be used as part of a Bash variable name, so we used the rather long name of $NOTEPAD_PLUS_PLUS instead. After you have sourced your .bashrc file in all open Bash windows, then whenever you wish to run Notepad++, you can type

```
$ notepad++ file_name &
```

at the Bash prompt. As with use of gVim, I recommend running Notepad++ in the background, so that you can still use your Bash window while the editor is running. There is no reason why you can't have both gVim and Notepad++ installed on your machine and even use them at the same time. In this case, the $PATH variable in .bashrc would look like

```
PATH="${PATH}:${VIM}:${NOTEPAD_PLUS_PLUS}"
export PATH
```

After sourcing the .bashrc file to make your changes take effect, you can now type different editor commands into the same Bash window:

```
$ notepad++ addresses.txt &
[1] 6056

$ gvim kitties.txt &
[2] 6332
```

You can also use job control to see just how many background processes the current Bash window is running:

```
$ jobs
[1]-  Running                notepad++ addresses.txt &
[2]+  Running                gvim kitties.txt &
```

Sublime Text 2

One of the newer and more popular editors is Sublime Text 2. While this version of the editor is currently free for unlimited evaluation, it may eventually require a paid license. As you should expect by now, this editor is also pretty easy to install and configure for use in Bash. Download the software from

```
http://www.sublimetext.com/2
```

After downloading the installer, double-click on it and you'll see a Windows security warning:

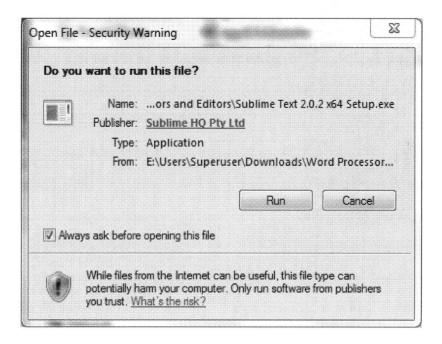

Click 'Yes' to continue. You'll then get the Setup dialog:

Click on 'Next' to continue. You'll get an opportunity to change the location where the software should be installed:

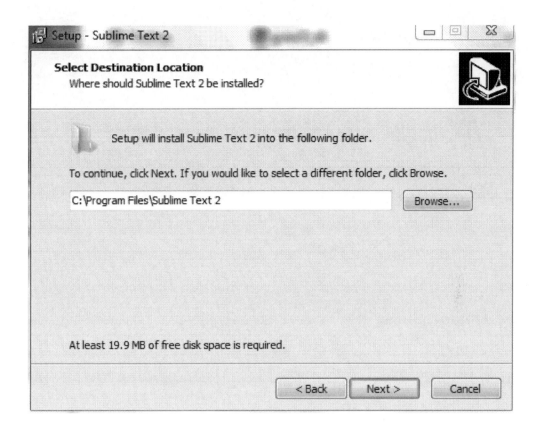

Click on 'Next' to continue. You can add the editor to the Windows Explorer menu by checking the checkbox in the next dialog:

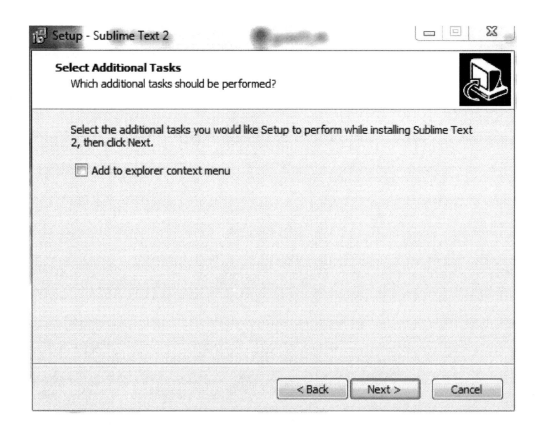

Again click on 'Next' to continue. This is your last chance to make changes before the installation begins:

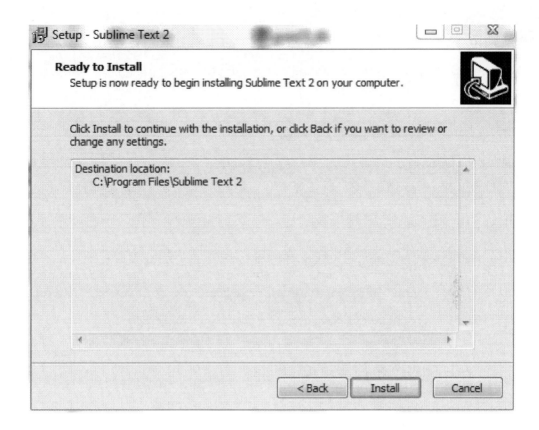

Click on 'Install' to run the installation. Afterward, you will see a notice that the installation is complete.

Click on 'Finish' to get out of the installer program. Strangely, even though the final dialog says

```
The application may be launched by selecting the
installed icons.
```

the installer doesn't seem to create a desktop shortcut for launching the editor. Instead, if you want to launch it from Windows, you'll have to choose 'Start->All Programs->Sublime Text 2.' To launch it from Git Bash, you will need to add the following lines to your .bashrc file:

```
SUBLIME_TEXT_2="/c/Program Files/Sublime Text 2"

PATH="${PATH}:${SUBLIME_TEXT2}"
```

```
export PATH
```

After saving your changes and sourcing the .bashrc file in all open Bash windows, you can now invoke the editor by typing

```
$ sublime_text file_name &
```

If that seems like more typing than you might prefer, you could also add an alias to your .bashrc file:

```
#  Note that variables have to be double-quoted inside the single quotes of
#  an alias.
alias st2='"{SUBLIME_TEXT_2}"/sublime_text.exe'
```

Once the alias is defined (after sourcing your .bashrc file again), you can then type

```
$ st2 file_name &
```

to start the editor. As we did with other editors, it is good to start Sublime Text 2 in the background by adding the ampersand to the end of the command line. This enables you to continue using your Bash window while you do your edits in the Sublime Text 2 window.

Using Ruby from Git Bash

Using your favorite programming language from Bash is also pretty straightforward once you have installed it; the most important thing is to tell Bash where the executable for your compiler or interpreter is. If, for example, we installed Ruby 1.9.2 on our system to the directory '/c/Ruby192/bin,' we would add the following lines to the .bashrc file:

```
RUBY_BIN='/c/Ruby192/bin'

PATH="${PATH}:${RUBY_BIN}"
export PATH
```

You may also wish to add an additional line to your .bashrc to make it easier to use the Interactive RuBy (IRB) environment directly from Bash:

```
#  This alias is needed because of a bug in Git Bash or Ruby, such that
#  when in the irb environment, the backspace key doesn't work properly.

alias irb='ruby -S irb'
```

If the above line is present in your .bashrc, you can then invoke irb by typing

```
$ irb
irb(main):001:0>
```

After typing in all the Ruby commands you wish to execute at the irb prompt, you can type 'exit' to get out when you are done.

Unless you are just testing out a few code snippets, it normally makes more sense to store the code in a text file with your favorite editor, and simply run it after each time you save new changes to the file. If you keep an open window with your source file, then each time you make a change to the file and save it, you can then run that program directly from the Bash command line without need of the interactive environment. (Your Bash window needs to be set to the same directory that contains your program source code.)

As an example, a simple Ruby program is shown on the next page:

```
#!/usr/bin/env ruby

#       FILE:   hello.rb
#       --------
#
#       The requisite "Hello, world" program.

puts "Hello from Ruby."
```

To run it, you can type

```
$ ruby hello.rb
Hello from Ruby.
```

But if you make sure the file is executable via the 'chmod' command,

```
$ chmod +x hello.rb
```

you can run it just by typing the file name:

```
$ hello.rb
Hello from Ruby.
```

This works because the 'shebang' line at the beginning of the script tells Bash that it is trying to execute a Ruby script.

Using Python from Git Bash

Using Python from Git Bash is even easier than using Ruby. Just add the following lines to your .bashrc file (assuming that you installed Python 2.7 to a directory named '/c/Python27'):

```
PYTHON_BIN='/c/Python27'

PATH="${PATH}:${PYTHON_BIN}"
export PATH
```

After you re-source .bashrc in all open Bash windows, you can now start up Python's interactive environment by simply typing

```
$ python
Python 2.7.1 (r271:86832, Nov 27 2010, 17:19:03) [MSC
v.1500 64 bit (AMD64)] on
win32
Type "help", "copyright", "credits" or "license" for more
information.
>>>
```

Type

```
>>> exit()
```

to exit. (Don't type '>>>,' which is the interactive prompt for Python.) If you have some code in a Python script, you can run it by typing, for example,

```
$ python hello.py
Hello, world.
```

This executes the code directly in Bash and does not make use of the interactive Python environment.

If our Python script looks like the one shown on the following page,

```
#!/usr/bin/env python

#     FILE:  hello.py
#     --------
#
#     The requisite "Hello, world" program.

print "Hello, world."
```

then once we make sure that the script is executable with the following command

```
$ chmod +x hello.py
```

we can run it simply by typing

```
$ hello.py
Hello, world.
```

As with our Ruby script, this works because the 'shebang' line at the beginning of the script tells Bash that we are trying to execute a Python script. Note that the 'chmod' command only needs to be run once to give the file the correct permissions.

Using the XAMPP LAMP Stack from Git Bash

XAMPP is one of the more popular LAMP (Linux Apache MySQL PHP) stacks available. It contains everything you need to do Web development in PHP or Perl, including the MySQL relational database and the Apache Web server. It also includes a number of extra utilities, including phpMyAdmin, which allows you to administer MySQL databases from a graphical user interface. The files included with your XAMPP download are arranged in a very specific directory structure:

```
C:\xampp
C:\xampp\apache\bin
C:\xampp\FileZillaFTP
C:\xampp\mysql\bin
C:\xampp\perl\bin
C:\xampp\php
C:\xampp\phpMyAdmin
```

Note that this software is not installed in 'C:\Program Files' by default. Although we used Windows path notation for the directories listed above, to get access to all the provided utilities, you'll need to reference them with Bash-style paths in your .bashrc file. First, add a definition like

```
XAMPP='/c/xampp'
```

Then add definitions that use the above variable:

```
APACHE_BIN="${XAMPP}/apache/bin"
FILEZILLA="${XAMPP}/FileZillaFTP"
MYSQL_BIN="${XAMPP}/mysql/bin"
XAMPP_PERL_BIN="${XAMPP}/perl/bin"
PHP="${XAMPP}/php"
```

Finally, you will need to add the last set of variables to your $PATH definition:

```
PATH="${PATH}:${APACHE_BIN}:${FILEZILLA}:${MYSQL_BIN}:$
```

```
{XAMPP_PERL_BIN}:${PHP}"
export PATH
```

After re-sourcing .bashrc in all open Bash windows, you can now use the above utilities from the command line if you wish. However, you may wish to define some additional aliases in your .bashrc file to simplify how much typing you have to do. For example, I can start and stop MySQL from the command line with aliases like

```
alias start_mysql='"C:\Program Files\MySQL\MySQL Server
5.5\bin\mysqld" &'
alias  stop_mysql='"C:\Program Files\MySQL\MySQL Server
5.5\bin\mysqladmin" -u root shutdown'  #  Add -p if a
root password is used
```

(Note that you may need to modify the above lines depending on which version of MySQL was included with your copy of XAMPP.) If you wish, you can also define an alias to start the XAMPP control panel from Bash (even though there is a desktop icon to do it from Windows):

```
alias start_xampp="${XAMPP}/xampp-control"
```

GNU on Windows: More Goodies You Can Run from Bash

There are other providers of GNU utilities that can run on Windows. You can use these programs as a supplement to or alternative to the Git Bash shell and its included utilities. One such alternative is the GNU on Windows project ('GoW' for short), which bills itself as "The lightweight alternative to Cygwin." You can get the software here:

```
https://github.com/bmatzelle/gow/wiki
```

A Windows installer is provided, and you can run the installed utilities directly from cmd.exe if you wish. However, with the proper setup you can also run many of these utilities from the Git Bash shell!

When you see that the GNU on Windows project provides 112 GNU utilities, you may wonder if you need Git Bash at all. The answer is, "it depends." GoW does provide a version of the Bash shell, but it is version 2.x, so it is even older than the version of Bash provided with Git. I don't recommend using it, especially since it seems to hang if you try to start it from Git Bash. You'll see that there is a lot of overlap between the GoW utilities and those of the Git Bash environment. My advice is to stick with the utilities provided with Git, except for those utilities that are unique to the GoW distribution. 68 of the GoW utilities are not included in the Git Bash distribution; here is a list:

```
bc
bzip2recover
chgrp
chown
chroot
cksum
clear.bat
csplit
dc
dd
df
diff3
```

expand
factor
fgrep
fmt
fold
gfind
gow.bat
gow.vbs
gsar
hostid
hostname
indent
install
join
jwhois
lesskey
make
mkfifo
mknod
ncftp
nl
od
pageant
paste
pathchk
plink
pr
printenv
pscp
psftp
putty
puttygen
scp.bat
sdiff
seq
sftp.bat
sha1sum
shar
ssh.bat

```
su
sum
sync
tac
test
unexpand
unix2dos
unlink
unrar
unshar
uudecode
uuencode
wget
whereis.bat
whoami
yes
zip
```

For example, the 'curl' utility, which allows you to retrieve Web pages from the command line, is included with Git Bash. Another popular utility that does the same type of thing is 'wget,' which is not provided by your Git installation. It is available in the GoW distribution, so if you really prefer that program, you might as well use it.

Git includes the 'diff' program for showing differences between two files, with lines from the first file displayed above lines from the second file. I have always liked the 'sdiff' program, which displays the same kind of differences, but shows them directly side-by-side. Git doesn't include 'sdiff,' but the GoW distribution does. (GNU diff does provide options for doing side-by-side differences, so you don't technically need sdiff. However, using sdiff requires less typing.)

You can access the GNU on Windows utilities from Git Bash by placing lines like the following in your .bashrc file:

```
PROGRAM_FILES_X86='/c/Program Files (X86)'

#  GNU on Windows utilities

GOW_BIN="${PROGRAM_FILES_X86}/gow/bin"

PATH="${PATH}:${GOW_BIN}"
```

```
export PATH
```

As usual, source .bashrc in all open Bash windows. Alternatively, you can exit each window and start a new one. Now you can use any of the GNU on Windows utilities that aren't included in the Git distribution simply by typing a command. For example,

```
$ wget http://www.google.com/
SYSTEM_WGETRC = c:/progra~1/wget/etc/wgetrc
syswgetrc = c:\Program Files (X86)\gow/etc/wgetrc
--2014-03-24 11:38:29--  http://www.google.com/
Resolving www.google.com... 74.125.224.209,
74.125.224.212, 74.125.224.210, ...
Connecting to www.google.com|74.125.224.209|:80...
connected.
HTTP request sent, awaiting response... 200 OK
Length: unspecified [text/html]
Saving to: `index.html'

    [ <=>                                        ] 11,505
--.-K/s    in 0s

2014-03-24 11:38:29 (205 MB/s) - `index.html' saved
[11505]
```

Note that because /bin appears in your $PATH variable before the definition of $GOW_BIN, any utilities that are common to Git and GoW will have the Git version found first. This is normally what you want, but if you have some reason to prefer one of the GoW utilities, you can always define an alias for it. (You could also just copy it into the /bin directory and overwrite the Git version of the program. I don't recommend doing this, though, because if you install a new version of Git, the contents of /bin may be replaced.)

You'll have to decide for yourself which utilities might be of use to you. There are some utilities that are convenient for using in Bash scripts. For example, the 'nl' utility provides an easy way to add line numbers to files:

```
$ nl kitties.txt
     1  When the cat's away, the mice will play.
     2  Two cats are better than one cat.
     3  My youngest cat quickly becomes thoroughly
```

```
      4  catatonic and listless after
      5  eating a big bowl of catnip.

      6  Cat is a GNU utility that is rarely used by
      7  the cats in my neighborhood.
```

By default, it doesn't number empty lines, but you can easily make it number all lines of the body text with the '-ba' option:

```
$ nl -ba kitties.txt
      1  When the cat's away, the mice will play.
      2  Two cats are better than one cat.
      3  My youngest cat quickly becomes thoroughly
      4  catatonic and listless after
      5  eating a big bowl of catnip.
      6
      7  Cat is a GNU utility that is rarely used by
      8  the cats in my neighborhood.
```

An easy way to create sequences of numbers is with the 'seq' utility. The syntax is of one of the forms

```
$ seq LAST
$ seq FIRST LAST
$ seq FIRST INCREMENT LAST
```

where FIRST, LAST, and INCREMENT are numbers. If only LAST is used, FIRST and INCREMENT are 1 by default. If only FIRST and LAST are used, INCREMENT is 1 by default. For example,

```
$ seq 5 9
5
6
7
8
9

$ seq 1 .5 3
1
1.5
```

```
2
2.5
3
```

This utility originally made it easier to have for loops that iterated over a set of numbers, but you can do this in Bash without need of seq. A (slightly modified) example from Wikipedia shows how to do this:

```
for ((n=1; n<=11; n++))
do
    rm file$n
done
```

You may find other uses for seq.

Another utility that developers sometimes find handy is the 'od' (octal dump) utility. By default, it shows the contents of a file in octal format, but you can change this. The '-c' option lets you see the file in the form of characters. This can be useful for looking at strings contained in binary files, and even for text files is it useful for showing you exactly what line endings a given file uses. Let's look at the first few lines of our venerable 'kitties.txt' file with od:

```
$ od -c kitties.txt | head -5
0000000   W   h   e   n       t   h   e       c   a   t   '   s       a
0000020   w   a   y   ,       t   h   e       m   i   c   e       w   i
0000040   l   l       p   l   a   y   .  \r  \n   T   w   o       c   a
0000060   t   s       a   r   e       b   e   t   t   e   r       t   h
0000100   a   n       o   n   e       c   a   t   .  \r  \n   M   y
```

The '\r\n' (carriage return/linefeed) pairs show clearly that this file was created on a Windows system. The GoW utilities can serve as a great supplement to your Git Bash installation.

GnuWin: Even More Utilities You Can Run from Bash

If you *still* haven't gotten your fill of UNIX-style tools, you may also have some interest in the GnuWin project, which provides Windows installers for a variety of GNU utilities. Using these utilities is a little more involved, since there is a separate installer for each utility or group of utilities. The home page for the project is

```
http://gnuwin32.sourceforge.net/
```

You can click on the 'Packages' link in the left-hand column to see the page for downloading individual installers:

```
http://gnuwin32.sourceforge.net/packages.html
```

Alternatively, you can click on the 'Download All' link and then on the 'this software package' link, which will take you to an installer on SourceForge.net:

```
http://sourceforge.net/projects/getgnuwin32/files/
```

The drill for making these files accessible in Bash is the same as in the previous sections. First, define a Bash variable that contains the path where you installed your chosen utility. Then add that variable to your $PATH and re-source .bashrc in all open Bash windows (or close each window and open a new one). You should be able to this yourself now by peeking at the examples in the previous sections.

Unless you have very specialized requirements, you probably won't need most of the utilities that are unique to this project, but there is no harm in looking at it to see if there is anything that might be useful to you.

Miscellaneous Utilities Like jq for Reading JSON Files

You may occasionally come across non-GNU Linux utilities that have been ported to Windows. One recent example is the 'jq' utility. This tool makes it easy to extract data from JSON files. (JSON, or JavaScript Object Notation, has become a popular language-independent format for data transfer and storage.) The tool was written in portable C and is provided as a single binary file with no runtime dependencies. The jq home page is

```
http://stedolan.github.io/jq/
```

Click on the 'Download' link to get the executable. You can get documentation by clicking on the 'Tutorial' or 'Manual' links. Note that some of the pages display with the leftmost character cut off in Firefox. On my system, I created a special directory for miscellaneous utilities and saved the executable there. Then I added the following lines to my .bashrc file:

```
#  Other Bash utilities

OTHER_BIN='/c/Other_Bash_Utilities'

PATH="${PATH}:${OTHER_BIN}"
export PATH
```

Again, once you have re-sourced .bashrc or restarted your Bash windows, you can use this tool without having to type in a path. To confirm that it works, you can try one of the command lines from the jq tutorial to grab some data from Twitter:

```
$ curl 'http://search.twitter.com/search.json?
q=json&rpp=5&include_entities=true' | jq '.results[0]'
  % Total     % Received % Xferd  Average Speed    Time
Time      Time  Current
                                   Dload  Upload   Total
Spent    Left  Speed
100    156  100    156      0      0   1106        0 --:--:--
```

```
--:--:-- --:--:--    1248
null
```

Note that the curl command above is displayed on two lines because it is so long. You really need to type it out all on one line to get the proper result. Or, if you want to enter it on multiple lines, put a backslash before each time you hit the <Enter> key. Then Bash will interpret all the text you typed as being on one line.

The command requests some search results from Twitter and then pipes them into the jq utility to get the output formatted in a (relatively) readable fashion. It should look better on your own screen than the way it is shown here.

Basic Git

At long last we are ready to have some discussion of Git. Putting this topic near the end of the book was a very deliberate choice on my part, partly to emphasize that this is not really a book about Git (which deserves an entire volume in its own right), but also to give you enough background about the structure and philosophy of UNIX and Linux systems that you won't run screaming from the room at your first taste of Git. Git was designed very much in line with the philosophy of all other Linux tools, and as a result it has a huge number of options that will take a significant amount of time to learn. The good news is that, even though Git has a steep learning curve, it is not that difficult to learn the most commonly used commands. In fact, you can see many of the available commands simply by typing

```
$ git
usage: git [--version] [--help] [-C <path>] [-c name=value]
           [--exec-path[=<path>]] [--html-path] [--man-path] [--info-path]
           [-p|--paginate|--no-pager] [--no-replace-objects] [--bare]
           [--git-dir=<path>] [--work-tree=<path>] [--namespace=<name>]
           <command> [<args>]

The most commonly used git commands are:
   add        Add file contents to the index
   bisect     Find by binary search the change that introduced a bug
   branch     List, create, or delete branches
   checkout   Checkout a branch or paths to the working tree
   clone      Clone a repository into a new directory
   commit     Record changes to the repository
   diff       Show changes between commits, commit and working tree, etc
   fetch      Download objects and refs from another repository
   grep       Print lines matching a pattern
   init       Create an empty Git repository or reinitialize an existing one
   log        Show commit logs
   merge      Join two or more development histories together
   mv         Move or rename a file, a directory, or a symlink
   pull       Fetch from and integrate with another repository or a local
branch

   push       Update remote refs along with associated objects
   rebase     Forward-port local commits to the updated upstream head
   reset      Reset current HEAD to the specified state
   rm         Remove files from the working tree and from the index
   show       Show various types of objects
   status     Show the working tree status
   tag        Create, list, delete or verify a tag object signed with GPG

'git help -a' and 'git help -g' lists available subcommands and some
```

```
concept guides. See 'git help <command>' or 'git help <concept>'
to read about a specific subcommand or concept.
```

We'll only cover some of these commands in this tutorial. See books on Git for details on the other commands.

Configuring Global Commands

Git wants very badly to keep track of who makes each change to each file. To do this, it would like every user of the system to record his or her identity. While this isn't strictly necessary, it much easier to work with Git if you enter this information right at the outset. Use commands like the following

```
$ git config --global user.name "Your_Name"
$ git config --global user.email "Your_EMail@Some_Company.com"
```

Naturally, you want to replace 'Your_Name' with your name, and 'Your_EMail@Some_Company.com' with your e-mail address. If you are working by yourself, you can set these to fake values if you like, but if you collaborate with others you will need to provide some real information.

Both of these parameters get stored in the file ~/.gitconfig. This is a human-readable file that can be examined and changed with any text editor. You can regard it as Git's equivalent to the .bashrc file.

Initializing a Repository

Creating a new Git repository is very easy. Start by switching to the top-level directory of your software project. Let's assume we're going to create a new 'bash_project' directory in our home directory. Then you would type

```
$ mkdir bash_project

$ cd bash_project

$ git init
Initialized empty Git repository in e:/Users/Michael
Hanna/bash_project/.git/
```

Once you have created a repository, you can try out the 'git status' command to check its state:

```
$ git status
On branch master

Initial commit

nothing to commit (create/copy files and use "git add" to
track)
```

All of the information about your repository will be stored in the 'hidden' .git directory that was just created by the 'git init' command. There are a couple of important points to consider. First, you can have multiple Git repositories, in any location in your file system. This can make keeping track of them all a little tricky. It is a good practice to decide on one or more standard locations for your Git repositories. If you lose track of a repository, you can search for it with with a command like

```
$ find . -name ".git" -type d -print
./.git
```

This searches for directories named '.git,' starting from the current location. (As you might expect, the current directory contains one and only one Git repository.)

The other important thing to be aware of is that *Git commands only work in a directory containing a repository (or one of its subdirectories)!* If you are in a location which doesn't have a .git directory in one of the parent directories, you will get an error message if you try to do a Git command; for example,

```
$ cd "$PROGRAM_FILES"

$ git status
fatal: Not a git repository (or any of the parent
directories): .git
```

Adding Files to the Staging Area/Index

When working with Git, there are actually three different locations where copies of your files may be found. The first is the normal directory where you created your file. This is commonly called your **working directory.** The second place is an invisible location called the **staging area** or **index.** This functions as a temporary holding area for files that you intend to store in the repository. You can place multiple files in the staging area, and if you change your mind about committing them to the repository, you can remove some or all of them from the staging area. When files in the staging area are committed to the repository, Git keeps track of who checked in which change and how the latest version of the file differs from the previous. (The underlying architecture is more complicated since Git actually deals with individual chunks of text called 'blobs' rather than entire files, but you don't need to know the details of how it works to be able to do basic Git operations.)

If you already have a set of source files in the directory where you created a repository, adding all the files to the index or staging area is as simple as typing

```
$ git add .
```

Note the period, which is Git-speak for "all files in the current directory." It is very similar to the '*' shell file glob. On a Windows system, you might occasionally see warnings like this,

```
$ git add .
warning: LF will be replaced by CRLF in LinuxBackup.
The file will have its original line endings in your
working directory.
```

but they aren't anything to be worried about. Git is just telling you that the line endings for your files will be stored differently in the repository than the original line endings in your working directory. Whether you see such messages depends on how you chose to deal with line endings during your installation of Git.

Once files have been added to the staging area, you can see the contents of the staging area by doing 'git status' again:

```
$ git status
On branch master
```

```
Initial commit

Changes to be committed:
  (use "git rm --cached <file>..." to unstage)

        new file:   for_loop_examples
        new file:   while_loop_examples
```

Committing Files

Committing files to the repository is equally easy, but there are two different ways to do it. One is to type a command like

```
$ git commit -m 'Initial revision.'
[master (root-commit) b323a07] Initial revision.
 2 files changed, 262 insertions(+)
 create mode 100644 for_loop_examples
 create mode 100644 while_loop_examples
```

This places all of the files in the staging area into the repository, and records the same **commit message** for each file. The purpose of the commit message is to summarize your changes to the file. Git prefers a summary of your change in the first 50 characters of the first line of your message. If you want to add additional text, Git prefers a blank line after the first one followed by any amount of additional text. Applying the same commit message to a bunch of files makes sense when you are checking them in for the first time, or when your files are logically related. For example, if you had to modify two files in order to fix a bug, you could check them in with a message like

```
$ git commit -m "Fixed bug #502."
```

If you need to write different messages for different files, just add the file names to the end of your commit command. For example,

```
$ git commit -m "Fixed bug #502" index.php help.php
$ git commit -m "Added site map" site_map.php
```

You can also commit all of the files in the index with the command

```
$ git commit
```

However, this adds a bit of complication. Git *always* wants you to enter a commit message, and will complain vociferously if you don't. If you give the commit command without the '-m' option, Git will automatically start up an editor to enable you to compose your commit message interactively. Git uses the Vim editor by default (and that is undoubtedly one of the reasons it is included in your installation of Git). When Vim starts up you will see a blank line at the top of the page (with the cursor at the beginning of the blank line) and text like this:

```
# Please enter the commit message for your changes. Lines starting
# with '#' will be ignored, and an empty message aborts the commit.
# On branch master
#
# Initial commit
#
# Changes to be committed:
#       new file:   for_loop_examples
#       new file:   while_loop_examples
#
```

This is excellent if you are a fervent fan of Vim like I am, but may be an instant stumbling block if you have never used this editor. If you find yourself in this situation, it is easy to add a simple message even if you don't know Vim.

Just type 'i' to insert or 'a' to append text. (Both commands effectively work the same way at the beginning of a new line of text.) Then type in your text and hit the escape key (<Esc>) to end text entry. Finally, you can type ':wq' to write the file and quit. (You *must* begin the file writing command with a colon.) After you quit the editor, Git will check in all of the files in the staging area and apply your commit message to each file in the list. That wasn't so bad, was it?

Setting a Default Editor

Some people get easily traumatized by Vim, because they expect every editor they use to be **modeless.** That is, they expect to be able to start typing text immediately without having to type any other commands first. Vim doesn't follow this paradigm (which actually has some great advantages, like allowing almost any key on the keyboard to be a command), but if you can't wrap your head around this, or simply don't have time to learn a new editor, you can configure Git to use a different editor instead. Let's look at a couple of examples of how to do this.

Setting Notepad++ as the Default Editor

If you followed the earlier instructions on how to install and configure Notepad++, the Notepad++ executable is already in your Bash $PATH variable. However, Git still needs to be told that you want to use this editor as your default for all Git operations that require an editor. You would normally do this with a command like

```
$ git config --global core.editor "'/c/Program Files
(x86)/Notepad++/notepad++.exe' -multiInst -notabbar
-nosession -noPlugin"
```

but because of the arcana of Git's quote handling, this doesn't work properly. Instead, it is easier to modify ~/.gitconfig directly and add text like

```
[core]
    editor = "'/C/Program Files (x86)/Notepad++/notepad+
+.exe' -multiInst -notabbar -nosession -noPlugin"
```

It is critical to note the placement of the quotation marks. The outer double quotes enclose the whole string, but the inner single quotes enclose *only* the path to the Notepad++ executable. You *don't* want to include the options to the command inside the single quotes. (The options bring up the editor without disturbing any of your other work.) After saving your changes, your next 'git commit' command will automatically invoke Notepad++. Type your commit message, save the file and quit, and Git will process your updates as usual.

Setting Sublime Text 2 as the Default Editor

You can set Sublime Text 2 as your default editor with the command

```
$ git config --global core.editor "sublime_text -n -w"
```

This works, but the '-n' flag was supposed to start the editor without using any previously open windows. On my system, it did open previous files in a separate window. Not that big a deal, but still a little annoying. (You can get rid of the window containing extraneous files by hitting <Alt-F4>.) This is not my primary editor, so I don't know how to fix this problem.

Creating a Label

Once you have created a major set of changes that comprise a whole release (or even just a new feature), you may want to apply a **label** to make it easy to refer to this release. In Git parlance, such a label is also known as a **tag,** since you use the 'git tag' command to create it. We can create a tag for the initial version of our software with the command

```
$ git tag -a V1.0 -m 'Initial release.'
```

If you don't use the '-m' option, Git will once again open your default editor and ask you to include a message describing the purpose of your tag. You'll note that we also used the '-a' option, which produces what Git calls an **annotated tag.** Git records the same type of information about who created the tag, when it was created, and what its purpose is, just as it would for any file that you check in. If you don't use the '-a' option, you get a regular tag in which this auxiliary information is not recorded. I strongly recommend *always* using the '-a' option to create annotated tags. In my opinion, this should be Git's default behavior.

Looking at Information in the Repository

Git has multiple commands for showing you the information that it tracks, and these commands have a bewildering variety of options. In some cases, two different command/option combinations can produce the same results. We'll only show a few examples here; you'll have to read the Git documentation if you want to know all the details of how these commands work.

We just learned how to create a tag to label a software release in the previous section, so let's learn how to view what tags are present in our repository. We can do this with the command

```
$ git tag -n1
V1.0            Initial release.
```

The '-n1' option says to produce one line of annotation from any annotated tags. If you leave out this option, you won't get the commit message for the tag:

```
$ git tag
V1.0
```

Most of the time, you will be interested in seeing what files have changed in the repository. The basic tool for getting this information is the 'git log' command. Without any options, you get multiple lines of output for each commit:

```
$ git log
commit b323a0743192bccf2f6533895e9274937f402ff2
Author: Michael Hanna <me@wherever.com>
Date:   Fri Apr 4 14:16:06 2014 -0700

    Initial revision.
```

The output starts with a long commit number, which is a unique 40-byte hash that is assigned to each change in the repository. Many Git commands can accept a particular commit number as input, but you should never need to type out the whole number. Typing a unique prefix of the number will suffice.

You can get a one-line-per-commit representation with the '--oneline' option:

```
$ git log --oneline
b323a07 Initial revision.
```

One problem with Git's commit-oriented way of thinking is that by default you don't see what files are involved in a group commit. One way to do this is with a command like

```
$ git log --name-status
commit b323a0743192bccf2f6533895e9274937f402ff2
Author: Michael Hanna <me@wherever.com>
Date:   Fri Apr 4 14:16:06 2014 -0700

    Initial revision.
```

```
A         for_loop_examples
A         while_loop_examples
```

The '--name-status' option shows only the name and status of the changed files. The initial 'A' to the left of the file names tells us that these were new files that were committed (added to the repository) for the first time.

You can also search for commits involving a specific file by listing the file name after all other options (the end of options is represented by '--'):

```
$ git log -- for_loop_examples
commit b323a0743192bccf2f6533895e9274937f402ff2
Author: Michael Hanna <me@wherever.com>
Date:   Fri Apr 4 14:16:06 2014 -0700

    Initial revision.
```

If you want to get fancier, you can even print out both the one commit we did and the tag that is associated with that commit

```
$ git log --oneline --decorate
b323a07 (HEAD, tag: V1.0, master) Initial revision.
```

HEAD is special Git notation that always refers to the latest commit.

You should also be aware that there is a 'git show' command, which by default shows the actual text of your source files that are associated with changes. This is usually more information than you want to see, but may sometimes come in handy.

Because Git commands have so many different options available, you can't get help from the command line. Instead, when you ask for help, Git launches a browser window or tab that takes you to the official online Git documentation. To get such information for the 'git show' command, you would type

```
$ git show --help
Launching default browser to display HTML ...
```

Whether you will actually *understand* the information in the Git help pages is a much different issue. You will probably be better off reading at least one of the books on Git before attempting to use the enormous array of command-line options that are available for each Git command.

Basic Branching

In addition to allowing you to track changes between individual files and allowing you to apply a tag to a whole release, Git also supports the concept of a **branch.** Branches can be used to distinguish whole sets of files (or releases) from one another. For example, after you finish the first version of your software (and create a 'V1.0' tag for it), you might need to continue fixing bugs in version 1.0 while you are also trying to develop new features for version 2.0. By creating a new branch for version 2.0, you can add new features to your product without disturbing the original 1.0 release.

In older revision control systems like CVS, creating a new branch was a very costly operation, because each new branch required making a physical copy of each file in the repository. This could eat up a huge amount of disk space for a large project. In Git however, the internal architecture is much more efficient, so massive copying is not needed to create a branch. This makes it much easier to use branching than in most other systems.

You can see what branches currently exist with the command

```
$ git branch
* master
```

The current branch is marked with an asterisk, and by default, you are considered to be on Git's master branch. When you want to create a new branch, choose an appropriate name (say, 'new_feature') and type

```
$ git branch new_feature
```

Then type

```
$ git checkout new_feature
Switched to branch 'new_feature'
```

Or you can do both commands in one step with the syntax

```
$ git checkout -b new_feature
```

Once you are in the new branch, you can edit any of your source files as needed, and use the 'git add' and 'git commit' commands to add your changes to the branch. These changes will *not* be visible from the master branch until you merge the new_feature branch into master. Let's assume that we add a new feature to one file. Then we can use the 'git log' command to confirm that the new feature was added:

```
$ git log --name-status
commit ddb50d91fda39d0e6e1e66301ec66927d992ada0
Author: Michael Hanna <me@wherever.com>
Date:   Sat Apr 5 01:29:48 2014 -0700

    Added a new feature.

M       while_loop_examples

commit 71d006792eb039e5fa7211e79ae9dd5a6d21912f
Author: Michael Hanna <me@wherever.com>
Date:   Fri Apr 4 16:29:42 2014 -0700

    Removed a comment.

M       while_loop_examples

commit b323a0743192bccf2f6533895e9274937f402ff2
Author: Michael Hanna <me@wherever.com>
Date:   Fri Apr 4 14:16:06 2014 -0700

    Initial revision.

A       for_loop_examples
A       while_loop_examples
```

If you switch back to the master branch again and do the same command, you will see that the new feature is not present on the master branch:

```
$ git checkout master
Switched to branch 'master'
```

```
$ !-2
git log --name-status
commit 71d006792eb039e5fa7211e79ae9dd5a6d21912f
Author: Michael Hanna <me@wherever.com>
Date:    Fri Apr 4 16:29:42 2014 -0700

     Removed a comment.

M          while_loop_examples

commit b323a0743192bccf2f6533895e9274937f402ff2
Author: Michael Hanna <me@wherever.com>
Date:    Fri Apr 4 14:16:06 2014 -0700

     Initial revision.

A          for_loop_examples
A          while_loop_examples
```

Note the use of the Bash history command '!-2' to repeat the previous 'git log' command. Bash doesn't care that we are in a different Git branch now; it just blindly repeats the previous command. But Git knows that we are in a different branch, so it applies the command to the master branch (which doesn't have the new feature).

The master branch is typically considered to be the **main line of descent** in the history of most projects. Once you have merged a branch back into the master (or decided that you no longer need the contents of the branch), you can get rid of it if you like by using the command

```
$ git branch -d new_feature
```

Basic Merging

When you wish to merge the code in a branch back into the main line of descent, you will need to use the 'git merge' command. There are conceptually two cases that you may need to deal with. In the first and simplest case, the code added in the branch is unique and doesn't change any lines of code that already exist in the master. Once you switch back to the master branch, you can easily integrate the new feature from your other branch with the command

```
$ git checkout master
Switched to branch 'master'

$ git merge new_feature
Updating 71d0067..ddb50d9
Fast-forward
 while_loop_examples | 2 ++
 1 file changed, 2 insertions(+)
```

In this case, Git is smart enough to add the new code to the master branch without any human assistance being needed. You won't always be so fortunate, however. If your new feature changes a line of code that already existed in the master branch, Git won't know which version of that code should take precedence. (Some might argue that the newest change should take precedence, but that isn't always correct.) If one version of your code says 'x = 2' and the other version says 'x = 3,' how is Git supposed to know which one you really want?

In a case like this, human judgment is required. If Git encounters this kind of scenario, it is known as a **merge conflict.** What Git does is to create a version of your file that contains *both* offending lines of code, with markers to indicate which line came from the master branch and which came from your new_feature branch. Your mission, should you choose to accept it, is to edit the file and *remove* whichever set of conflicting lines you *don't* wish to keep. Then do the usual 'git add' and 'git commit' commands to put the conflict-free version of the file into the master branch. While this sounds rather complicated, in practice it is usually not that difficult.

As an example, let's assume that we create another branch and once again edit the same shell script, though starting in the master branch. This time, we will change the script's exit command from 'exit 1' (failure) to 'exit 0' (success) in the master. We'll then go to the new conflict_branch and change that version of the file from 'exit 1' to 'exit 2.' When we return to the master branch and try to merge the changes, we'll get a merge conflict since the line of code we changed has a different value in both branches.

We start by creating the new branch, but we won't switch to it since we're going to edit the file in the master branch first:

```
$ git branch conflict_feature
```

Next, edit the file to use 'exit 0' instead of 'exit 1:'

```
$ gvim while_loop_examples &
```

You can see the results of the edit by using 'git diff' to compare the version of your file in the working directory to what is in the index:

```
$ git diff
diff --git a/while_loop_examples b/while_loop_examples
index 4ef7d5d..a9bf283 100644
--- a/while_loop_examples
+++ b/while_loop_examples
@@ -103,4 +103,4 @@ done

 #  Here is a new feature

-exit 1
+exit 0

$ git add while_loop_examples

$ git commit -m "Changed 'exit 1' to 'exit 0'"
[master 373aacf] Changed 'exit 1' to 'exit 0'
 1 file changed, 1 insertion(+), 1 deletion(-)
```

Now that we have changed a line in our file on the master branch, let's change the same line in the branch version of the file:

```
$ git checkout conflict_feature
Switched to branch 'conflict_feature'
```

In the branch version of the file, we change 'exit 1' to 'exit 2'. (I'm doing this just to generate a conflict, but sometimes you may want an unsuccessful script to have an exit status other than one, especially if there are multiple possible failure modes.)

```
$ gvim while_loop_examples &

$ git diff
diff --git a/while_loop_examples b/while_loop_examples
```

```
index 4ef7d5d..16286c3 100644
--- a/while_loop_examples
+++ b/while_loop_examples
@@ -103,4 +103,4 @@ done

 #  Here is a new feature

-exit 1
+exit 2
```

Now we add and commit the change to the branch:

```
$ git add while_loop_examples

$ git commit -m "Changed 'exit 1' to 'exit 2'"
[conflict_feature 27f4a52] Changed 'exit 1' to 'exit 2'
 1 file changed, 1 insertion(+), 1 deletion(-)
```

Next, let's return to the master branch and try to merge conflict_branch into the master. Note that it is a good practice to use 'git status' to make sure that your directory has no pending changes before you attempt a merge.

```
$ git checkout master
Switched to branch 'master'

$ git merge conflict_feature
Auto-merging while_loop_examples
CONFLICT (content): Merge conflict in while_loop_examples
Automatic merge failed; fix conflicts and then commit the
result.
```

Oops, we just got notified of a merge conflict. Happily, 'git diff' operates in a special way during merges, so that it will directly show you the merge conflicts in its output:

```
$ git diff
diff --cc while_loop_examples
index a9bf283,16286c3..0000000
--- a/while_loop_examples
+++ b/while_loop_examples
```

```
@@@ -103,4 -103,4 +103,8 @@@ don

  #  Here is a new feature

++<<<<<<< HEAD
 +exit 0
++=======
+ exit 2
++>>>>>>> conflict_feature
```

If you look at the file in a text editor, you'll see that these same lines are present (without the leading plus signs):

```
#  Here is a new feature

<<<<<<< HEAD
exit 0
=======
exit 2
>>>>>>> conflict_feature
```

What you need to do in your editor is choose which line of code you want to use in the master branch. Then you need to delete the other line, and you must delete all the merge conflict markers as well. (The merge conflict markers won't be recognized as proper code by Bash or most other programming languages. Worse yet, if they were recognized, they would mess up the operation of your program.) So you must delete the lines beginning with '<<<,' '===,' and '>>>.' In our case, let's keep the traditional 'exit 0' line and remove everything else between the merge conflict markers, so that the file looks like this:

```
#  Here is a new feature

exit 0
```

Now save your work and add it to the repository like a normal change:

```
$ git add while_loop_examples
```

When you commit the file, Git will be aware that you are doing a merge and give you appropriate messages.

```
$ git commit

Merge branch 'conflict_feature'

Conflicts:
        while_loop_examples
#
# It looks like you may be committing a merge.
# If this is not correct, please remove the file
#       .git/MERGE_HEAD
# and try again.


# Please enter the commit message for your changes. Lines starting
# with '#' will be ignored, and an empty message aborts the commit.
# On branch master
# All conflicts fixed but you are still merging.
#
```

Enter your commit message as usual, and use ':wq' to save your changes and exit (if you are using Vim as your default editor). Alternatively, you can include your commit message with your commit command:

```
$ git commit -m "Merged conflict_feature into master branch."
[master 763a60b] Merged conflict_feature into master branch.
```

Git: Attack of the Clones

The 'git clone' command provides an easy way to duplicate the contents of an entire repository, including its entire commit history. There are two common cases where you might want to use it: One is duplicating an existing hosted repository, such as a project on GitHub. The other case is making a copy of one of your own local repositories. Note that once you have cloned a repository, **you do not need to do the 'git clone' command again.** Doing so will completely overwrite your copy of the repository. Instead, we'll use the 'git pull' command (discussed soon) to keep it up to date.

Let's start with the case of cloning an existing project from GitHub. For example, suppose you wanted to clone the jQuery repository into a directory in your home directory. The command to do this is

```
$ git clone git://github.com/jquery/jquery.git
```

This will put a copy of the repository into the directory ~/jquery. If you want to clone the repository to a different directory name, just add the directory after the URL for the project you want to clone. Let's try cloning to a directory like 'customized_jquery' by following these steps:

```
$ cd
```

```
$ git clone git://github.com/jquery/jquery.git customized_jquery
Cloning into 'customized_jquery'...
remote: Reusing existing pack: 32992, done.
remote: Total 32992 (delta 0), reused 0 (delta 0)
Receiving objects: 100% (32992/32992), 19.39 MiB | 733.00 KiB/s,
done.
Resolving deltas: 100% (23383/23383), done.
Checking connectivity... done.
```

You don't have to create the new 'customized_jquery' directory beforehand; the clone command will do it for you. You can look at the directory afterward to confirm that it now contains a .git directory and a bunch of source files:

```
$ cd customized_jquery
```

```
$ ls -aF
./                .gitattributes  .mailmap         Gruntfile.js      package.json
../               .gitignore      .npmignore       MIT-LICENSE.txt   src/
.bowerrc          .jscs.json      .travis.yml      README.md         test/
.editorconfig     .jshintignore   AUTHORS.txt      bower.json
.git/             .jshintrc       CONTRIBUTING.md  build/
```

Git communicates with repositories on other machines by using a shorthand notation called a **remote.** When you clone an existing repository, Git will create remotes for you. You can see the existing remotes for the jQuery repository with the command

```
$ git remote -v
origin  git://github.com/jquery/jquery.git (fetch)
origin  git://github.com/jquery/jquery.git (push)
```

The remote name is used for pushing data to and pulling data from the repository. For example, if you want to pull down any new changes to jQuery from GitHub, do the command

```
$ git pull origin
```

```
Already up-to-date.
```

In reality, 'origin' is the default name for a remote, so you can usually just type

```
$ git pull
Already up-to-date.
```

Git can also be used to clone a repository on your local machine. This is one way of backing up a repository. (Though you should do normal system backups too.) As a simple example, let's clone the 'bash_project' directory:

```
$ cd
```

```
$ git clone bash_project bash_project_backup
Cloning into 'bash_project_backup'...
done.
```

It is easy to confirm that the local clone operation worked:

```
$ cd bash_project_backup
```

```
$ ls -aF
./   ../   .git/   for_loop_examples*   while_loop_examples*
```

Note that cloning a repository really only creates a snapshot of the repository *at one moment in time*. When you make changes to the original repository, you will need to periodically update your clone of the repository by using the 'git pull' command. One of the things that the 'git clone' command did was to create a remote repository reference. By default, this reference is named 'origin' and that name is associated with the path to the original repository. When you do a pull in the cloned repository, you use syntax like

```
$ git pull [remote-repository-name]
```

or, using the default name,

```
$ git pull origin
```

In fact, Git will use the 'origin' reference by default, so 'git pull' is all you normally need. Let's go to the original repository, make a change to it, and then do a pull in the clone to make sure it stays up to date. Remember that Git is context-sensitive; you must switch to the clone directory first and then do the pull. Never try to do a pull from the original project directory.

```
$ cd ~/bash_project

$ gvim while_loop_examples &

$ git add while_loop_examples

$ git commit -m "Add a final output message."
[master 6d0886e] Add a final output message.
 1 file changed, 2 insertions(+)

$ cd ~/bash_project_backup

$ git pull
remote: Counting objects: 7, done.
remote: Compressing objects: 100% (3/3), done.
remote: Total 3 (delta 2), reused 0 (delta 0)
Unpacking objects: 100% (3/3), done.
From e:/Users/Michael Hanna/bash_project
   763a60b..6d0886e  master      -> origin/master
Updating 763a60b..6d0886e
Fast-forward
 while_loop_examples | 2 ++
 1 file changed, 2 insertions(+)
```

Now the clone once again has all of the changes that are in the original. You'll need to do similar updates when using a master repository to collaborate with other people. If you have a whole bunch of repositories that you need to back up and update regularly, you could put the commands for these operations into a Bash shell script and run it whenever you want to do updates. (Linux users could even use the 'cron' utility to run the script at specified time intervals.)

Setting Up a Remote Repository for Collaborating with Others

If you have been following the examples so far, you have already created a local repository in your home directory. I'll use the 'bash_project' repository created earlier for this example. You can use any other repository that you prefer; just be sure to type its name rather than 'bash_project' in the instructions that follow.

Our goal here is to take the initial repository that we created and place it on a hosting service that will make it available to authorized users anywhere over the Internet. We'll assume that there is one other friend of yours who wants to work on your project, and that you both want to have a master repository on a hosting service so you can easily share your work. For convenience, I'll assume that your friend will work in a clone of the master repository on the same machine where the original was created, but the instructions should work just as well for someone on a different (Windows) system, no matter where in the world it is located.

One complication is that there are a variety of hosting services for source code repositories, and all of them work slightly differently. So we'll have to pick one and do instructions for that. You may need to modify the instructions to some degree to be compatible with other hosting systems. We'll assume that you would prefer to use a free hosting service rather than one that charges a monthly subscription fee. Happily, there are several free hosting services available (though they may have limits on the numbers of users, the amount of disk space you can use, or other constraints). Here are several such sites:

```
https://bitbucket.org/
```

```
http://bettercodes.org/
```

```
http://codebreak.com/
```

For this book, I'll choose Bitbucket, since not only are they free for up to five users, their site has good documentation as well (always a good sign for new users). To get started with Bitbucket, you'll need to go to their home page and create a new account. You'll need to create a unique username up to 30 characters long, you'll need to provide an e-mail address that will be unique across the whole Bitbucket site, and a password up to 128 characters long. I'm not going to give you my real account data, so let's assume for this discussion that we chose the following values:

```
Username:  DarthVader
E-Mail Address:  darth@deathstar.com
Password:  come_over_to_the_dark_side!!
```

Click on the "Create your first repository" button. On the "Create a new repository" page, you'll need to enter the name of the repository. This name will be included in the project's URL, so it must follow the rules for creating URLs. I used the name 'bash_project.' You'll need to enter a short description of the project as well. Leave the box checked for it to be a private repository. The project type should of course be 'Git.' Don't bother to check either of the project management checkboxes unless you wish to experiment with Bitbucket's software for issue tracking or its wiki. (We won't cover those here.) Finally, click on the "Create repository" button. Bitbucket will create a new, empty repository for you.

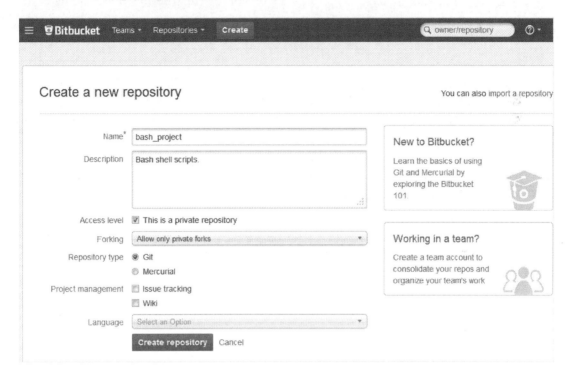

Hosting services actually create a special type of Git repository, called a **bare repository**. A bare repository contains the .git directory and all the internal data that Git uses to track commits, but doesn't include working copies of any files in the repository. Even after you upload commits to Bitbucket, its repository won't have any working copies of the files you committed, so you won't be able to view them directly.

Now you'll find yourself on the "Add some code" page. Here you get two choices:

I'm starting from scratch
I have an existing project to push up

Pushing to and Pulling from Remote Repositories

Continuing use of our repository on Bitbucket from the previous section, we'll click on the second link since we have an existing project. This will send you to the "Push up an existing repository" page. This page gives you the instructions that you need to type into a Bash window on your local computer to upload your existing repository to Bitbucket. I have modified these instructions for our chosen username and project name:

```
cd ~/bash_project
git remote add origin https://DarthVader@bitbucket.org/DarthVader/bash_project.git
git push -u origin --all # pushes up the repo and its refs for the first time
git push -u origin --tags # pushes up any tags
```

Naturally, if your repository is named something other than 'bash_project,' substitute the appropriate name, both in the cd command and in the URL. Similarly, you'll need to change 'DarthVader' to your actual username. Before doing the Git commands, it's a good idea to do 'git status' first to make sure your repository has no pending changes. When you actually type in the commands, you should see results like this:

```
$ cd ~/bash_project

$ git status
On branch master
nothing to commit, working directory clean

$ git remote add origin
https://DarthVader@bitbucket.org/DarthVader/bash_project.
git

$ git push -u origin --all
Password for 'https://DarthVader@bitbucket.org':
Counting objects: 21, done.
Delta compression using up to 4 threads.
Compressing objects: 100% (21/21), done.
Writing objects: 100% (21/21), 3.17 KiB | 0 bytes/s,
done.
```

```
Total 21 (delta 11), reused 0 (delta 0)
To
https://DarthVader@bitbucket.org/DarthVader/bash_project.
git
 * [new branch]      conflict_feature -> conflict_feature
 * [new branch]      master -> master
 * [new branch]      new_feature -> new_feature
Branch conflict_feature set up to track remote branch
conflict_feature from orig
in.
Branch master set up to track remote branch master from
origin.
Branch new_feature set up to track remote branch
new_feature from origin.
```

After you have done these commands, you can go back to the "Push up an existing repository page" in your Web browser and click on the "Next" button. This will take you to the "Make changes and push" page. At this point, your repository has been successfully uploaded into the empty repository you created on the Bitbucket site. There are now two copies of your repository, one on your local machine, and one on the Bitbucket hosting service. We are going to use the copy on Bitbucket as the 'official' authoritative copy of the repository that you and any other people on the project will use. What happens the next time you make a change to your local repository?

If you change your local repository, it will be out of synchronization with the 'official' version of the repository. So you will need to upload your changes to the Bitbucket repository to keep it up to date. The "Make changes and push" page provides an overview of how to do this. We will add a new file to the original repository on our local machine, and then push it up to Bitbucket. Here is the code for the sample script,

```
#!/bin/env bash

#      FILE:  update_bash_project_backup
#      --------------------------
#
#      Update the cloned copy of the 'bash_project'
repository.
```

```
ORIGINAL_REPOSITORY="~/bash_project"
BACKUP_REPOSITORY="~/bash_project_backup"

cd "$BACKUP_REPOSITORY"

git pull

exit 0
```

This script updates the local clone of bash_project that we created earlier. The script operates on the local machine only, so it doesn't care about what code is on Bitbucket. However, because we are going to check the code into the bash_project repository, and we want all such changes to be reflected in Bitbucket's copy of the repository, information about this script will be sent to Bitbucket, even if the script is never intended to be run on the Bitbucket site. Here is how we check the file in and upload the changes to Bitbucket:

```
cd ~/bash_project

$ gvim update_bash_project_backup &

$ git add update_bash_project_backup

$ git commit -m "Simple script to update the cloned
repository."
[master ade7eac] Simple script to update the cloned
repository.
 1 file changed, 15 insertions(+)
 create mode 100644 update_bash_project_backup

$ git push -u origin master
Password for 'https://DarthVader@bitbucket.org':
Counting objects: 6, done.
Delta compression using up to 4 threads.
Compressing objects: 100% (3/3), done.
Writing objects: 100% (3/3), 523 bytes | 0 bytes/s, done.
Total 3 (delta 0), reused 0 (delta 0)
To
```

```
https://DarthVader@bitbucket.org/DarthVader/bash_project.
git
    6d0886e..ade7eac  master -> master
Branch master set up to track remote branch master from
origin.
```

Now the Bitbucket repository has a copy of our new shell script, but what happens when a new user joins the project and needs to get his or her own copy of the 'official' repository on Bitbucket? This is exactly like the situation we described earlier for grabbing an existing repository from GitHub. The new user will need the password to your Bitbucket account since we made the official repository private. (Alternatively, you can click the 'Send invitation' button on your dashboard the next time you log into Bitbucket to send an e-mail request for your friend to join Bitbucket as a separate user.) Your collaborator can use the 'git clone' command as usual; just be sure to enter it on one line instead of the three shown here:

```
$ git clone
https://DarthVader@bitbucket.org/DarthVader/bash_project.
git bash_project_2nd_user
Cloning into 'bash_project_2nd_user'...
Password for 'https://DarthVader@bitbucket.org':
remote: Counting objects: 24, done.
remote: Compressing objects: 100% (24/24), done.
remote: Total 24 (delta 11), reused 0 (delta 0)
Unpacking objects: 100% (24/24), done.
Checking connectivity... done.
```

The second user can now make changes to his/her own local repository and push changes to the main repository on Bitbucket as needed.

However, there is one key change in your habits that you need to make when sharing a repository with multiple collaborators: **Always pull from the main repository before you attempt to push your local changes.** Why is this necessary? To understand why, consider what happens when two people modify the same part of the same file in each of their local repositories. One person pushes his change to the main repository on Bitbucket, but then the second person tries to push her change as well. As you might expect, the second attempt to push a change to the same part of the same file results in a **merge conflict.** When a merge conflict occurs, Git inserts conflict markers into the working copies of the files that conflict. But the repository on Bitbucket is a bare repository; it doesn't have any working copies of the files involved, so it has no place to put the merge conflict information for human use! Thus, the conflict can't be resolved on Bitbucket; instead, it has to be resolved in one of the local repositories that has working copies of the files (in this case, the second user's local repository).

What the second user should have done is to type

```
$ git pull
```

before attempting to push any changes. Then the second user would have gotten a merge conflict message, and would have merge conflict markers in her own local copy of the file that conflicted. She would then edit the file locally, decide which changes to keep, remove the conflict markers, save the file, add it to Git and commit it, and *then* do

```
$ git push -u origin master
```

This time the push would succeed without any problems. If you make a habit of always pulling from your main repository (and resolving any merge conflicts) before trying to push your local changes, your life with Git will run *much* more smoothly.

Using SSH to Connect to Remote Repositories

To get better security for your remote repository, you may wish to connect via SSH (the Secure SHell) rather than via the HTTPS protocol. SSH uses what is known as **public key cryptography** to authenticate users. Public key systems use a *pair* of keys, one of which is private, and one of which is public. The user keeps the private key on his or her own computer (or even on a flash drive), but gives a copy of the public key to the remote system. This allows the remote system to verify who you are in a more secure fashion than just using a regular password. We will again use Bitbucket as our example of a remote system to connect to, so some of the instructions that follow will only apply to Bitbucket. We'll paraphrase some of Bitbucket's instructions, but you can check Bitbucket's Web site for more details.

First, verify that you actually have ssh installed correctly by typing

```
$ ssh -v
OpenSSH_4.6p1, OpenSSL 0.9.8e 23 Feb 2007
usage: ssh [-1246AaCfgkMNnqsTtVvXxY] [-b bind_address] [-c cipher_spec]
           [-D [bind_address:]port] [-e escape_char] [-F configfile]
           [-i identity_file] [-L [bind_address:]port:host:hostport]
           [-l login_name] [-m mac_spec] [-O ctl_cmd] [-o option] [-p port]
           [-R [bind_address:]port:host:hostport] [-S ctl_path]
           [-w local_tun[:remote_tun]] [user@]hostname [command]
```

If you don't see similar output, there is something seriously wrong with your Git installation, as ssh and the other tools that we'll use should be included in the /bin directory.

The ssh utility keeps its configuration information in the directory ~/.ssh. If you don't already have this directory on your local machine, you'll need to create it, using the commands

```
$ cd
```

```
$ mkdir .ssh
```

(Don't forget the period in front of the directory name!) You should also cd to that directory and list its contents. If you see files named 'id_rsa' and 'id_rsa.pub,' that means that you (or some other user of your system) has already created an SSH key pair. The file 'id_rsa.pub' is the default name for the public version of the key, and 'id_rsa' is the default name of the private key. If these files already exist, you can use the 'mv' command to rename them or temporarily move them to another directory.

Creating SSH Keys

Creating a pair of SSH keys is done on your local machine with the 'ssh-keygen' command. To generate a new pair of keys using the default file names, type

```
$ cd ~/.ssh

$ ssh-keygen -t rsa
Generating public/private rsa key pair.
Enter file in which to save the key (/e/Users/Michael
Hanna/.ssh/id_rsa):
Enter passphrase (empty for no passphrase):
Enter same passphrase again:
Passphrases do not match. Try again.
Enter passphrase (empty for no passphrase):
Enter same passphrase again:
Your identification has been saved in /e/Users/Michael
Hanna/.ssh/id_rsa.
Your public key has been saved in /e/Users/Michael
Hanna/.ssh/id_rsa.pub.
The key fingerprint is:
46:80:95:d4:71:f4:00:99:95:a2:d0:5b:e5:cf:ee:37 Michael
Hanna@MY_COMPUTER
```

When asked for the file in which to save the key, just hit <Enter> to accept the default. Next, you enter your chosen passphrase twice. (To reduce hassles, you can also hit <Enter> here to use no passphrase at all, but this will significantly reduce your security. Don't do this unless you are just experimenting.) Ideally, you should choose a long passphrase (say, more than 15-20 characters) with plenty of numbers and oddball characters in it. Unfortunately, such passwords can be very difficult to type, and almost impossible to memorize, so you'll have to decide on a compromise you can live with. **Be sure to write down your passphrase; if you lose it, there is no way to get it back!** Your only recourse will be to create a new pair of keys.

After the keys are created. you should see that the files 'id_rsa' and 'id_rsa.pub' are now present. If you don't wish to use the default file names, you can add the '-f' option to ssh-keygen:

```
$ ssh-keygen -t rsa -f bitbucket
Generating public/private rsa key pair.
Enter passphrase (empty for no passphrase):
Enter same passphrase again:
Your identification has been saved in bitbucket.
Your public key has been saved in bitbucket.pub.
The key fingerprint is:
dc:60:fd:7e:72:3d:16:25:40:81:cc:0f:78:e3:89:b3 Michael
Hanna@MY_COMPUTER
```

This time, you'll see the files 'bitbucket' and 'bitbucket.pub' in the .ssh directory.

Creating an SSH Configuration File

Next, you need to open a text editor and create the file ~/.ssh/config. If the file already exists, you'll just add the following lines to it:

```
Host bitbucket.org
 IdentityFile ~/.ssh/id_rsa
```

(If you chose to create a key called 'bitbucket,' you would use 'bitbucket' instead of 'id_rsa.') Be sure to indent the second line with at least a single space. When you are done, save the file. The lines that you added tell ssh where to find the proper private key file for authenticating a connection to the host bitbucket.org. The config file can contain multiple sets of commands like this showing how to connect to different hosts.

Installing the Public Key into Bitbucket

Now your local system is configured for using ssh to communicate with the Bitbucket host, but we still need to tell Bitbucket about your public key. Open your browser and log into your Bitbucket account. The first challenge is to find the user-unfriendly icon in the upper right corner of your browser window that looks vaguely like a human head and shoulders. This is a dropdown menu that you should click on, and then choose 'Manage Account.' Click on the 'SSH keys' link in the left column of the page. You'll see a bright blue 'Add key' button. Click on it and you will see two boxes, one to enter a label, and another larger box in which you will enter your public key. Enter whatever text you like for the label; I used 'Primary User.'

Next, your need to enter your public key. This is the tricky part. First, you need to return to your Git Bash window. In the .ssh directory, do the command

```
$ cat id_rsa.pub
```

You will see multiple lines of output, but keep in mind that your public key is effectively one line of text. Now you want to select that text and copy it to the Windows Clipboard. (Either use the 'Edit->Copy' menu choice from the Git Bash window, or if you configured the software as recommended in the beginning of the book, just hit <Enter> to place the selected text into the Windows Clipboard.) An alternative strategy to place the public key into the Windows Clipboard is to do the command

```
clip < ~/.ssh/id_rsa.pub
```

Note that clip is *not* one of the GNU utilities supplied with Git. It is actually a Windows command-line utility that places any text it is given into the Windows Clipboard. But it works fine from Git Bash and even lets you redirect its input to come from a file with the usual '<' Bash operator.

Now return to your browser window, click in the Bitbucket 'Key' box and use <Ctrl-v> to paste. After the text is pasted is when your trouble begins. Remember that the public key is supposed to be one line of text? It isn't any more. Windows added line endings when it pasted the text into the dialog box! You must carefully backspace to eliminate the end-of-line characters. Start from the bottom of the window. If you find that backspacing removes a character at the end of the previous line, re-type it. (Or better yet, use <Ctrl-z> to undo the previous change; namely, your accidental deletion of the character.) And when you make it up to the first line, note 'ssh-rsa' *must* have a space after it. I found that after backspacing and re-adding the space, the rest of the key was moved down to the next line.

After making sure that everything is correct, click on the 'Add key' button. It may seem like nothing happened. If so, scroll down and you'll probably see the following message in red:

```
Invalid SSH key (ssh-keygen).
```

This almost certainly means that you just made an error while trying to backspace over the end-of-line characters. Don't feel too frustrated; this type of thing has happened every single time I have entered a public key on a remote hosting service. You'd think that these services might automatically remove such characters from the key, but nobody that I know of does this. In the worst case, you'll have to re-paste the key into the box and start over. If you have never done it before, it may take you multiple tries to get it right. (I had to try half a dozen times or more to enter my key into Bitbucket.)

Once the key has been successfully accepted, Bitbucket will send you an e-mail confirming that the key was added, on the off chance that a hacker might have entered the key instead of you.

Testing the Connection

Now let's try to connect to Bitbucket using our key pair. Bitbucket recommends using the 'ssh -T' command to test the connection. The first time you try to connect, you'll see output like

```
$ ssh -T git@bitbucket.org
The authenticity of host 'bitbucket.org (131.103.20.167)'
can't be established.
RSA key fingerprint is
97:8c:1b:f2:6f:14:6b:5c:3b:ec:aa:46:46:74:7c:40.
Are you sure you want to continue connecting (yes/no)?
yes
Warning: Permanently added 'bitbucket.org,131.103.20.167'
(RSA) to the list of k
nown hosts.
Enter passphrase for key '/e/Users/Michael
Hanna/.ssh/id_rsa':
Connection closed by 131.103.20.167
```

You should answer 'yes' to continue connecting, since the RSA key fingerprint that is displayed matches that of Bitbucket's public key fingerprint listed in their documentation. This will result in adding 'bitbucket.org' as a known host. It appears that I mistyped the passphrase on the first try, thus causing the connection to be closed prematurely, so I had to try again:

```
$ !!
ssh -T git@bitbucket.org
Enter passphrase for key '/e/Users/Michael
Hanna/.ssh/id_rsa':
logged in as DarthVader.

You can use git or hg to connect to Bitbucket. Shell
access is disabled.
```

The connection finally worked after I managed to type in the passphrase correctly.

Configuring Bitbucket to Use SSH Instead of HTTPS

We have previously connected to Bitbucket using the HTTPS protocol, which requires entering a password each time we connect to the server. This method also requires that we configure Git to use URLs of the form

```
https://accountname@bitbucket.org/accountname/reponame.git
```

where 'accountname' in our case would be 'DarthVader' or whatever name you chose for your own account. If we use SSH to communicate with Bitbucket instead, there are two valid URL formats that you can use:

```
git@bitbucket.org:accountname/reponame.git
```

or

```
ssh://git@bitbucket.org/accountname/reponame.git
```

Where do we put this information so that Git will use the right protocol? We are *not* going to change ~/.gitconfig, which contains settings that apply to all our Git repositories. Instead, the easiest thing to do is to modify the config file for the specific repository that we have stored on Bitbucket. (This is yet another configuration file that is different from the ~/.ssh/config file we discussed earlier.) Git is flexible enough that you can change its configuration on a per-repository basis. Let's look at the config file for our repository, which resides inside the .git directory for that repository:

```
$ cd ~/bash_project/.git
```

```
$ ls -aF
./              HEAD          config        hooks/   logs/
../             ORIG_HEAD     description   index    objects/
COMMIT_EDITMSG  TAG_EDITMSG   gitk.cache    info/    refs/
```

```
$ gvim config &
```

After opening the file in your favorite editor (it doesn't have to be gVim), you'll see several lines like this near the middle of the file:

```
[remote "origin"]
        url = https://DarthVader@bitbucket.org/DarthVader/bash_project.git
        fetch = +refs/heads/*:refs/remotes/origin/*
```

Change the 'url =' line to either

```
url = git@bitbucket.org:DarthVader/bash_project.git
```

or

```
url = ssh://git@bitbucket.org/DarthVader/bash_project.git
```

where 'DarthVader' is replaced with your real account name, and 'bash_project' is replaced with whatever you chose to name your sample project. Then save your changes and quit the editor. Git should now be able to communicate with Bitbucket using the SSH protocol.

Connecting to a Remote Repository Via SSH

We'll follow the example in Bitbucket's documentation by adding a README file to our local repository and then pushing the changes in our repository to the copy of our repository hosted on Bitbucket. Our normal way of using Git should 'just work' since we have installed our SSH public key on Bitbucket, and we changed our local repository's configuration to use SSH:

```
$ cd ~/bash_project

$ cat > README
This Git repository contains example Bash shell scripts.
<Ctrl-d>

$ git add README

$ git commit -m "Making a change that will be sent to
Bitucket using SSH"
[master 8307de9] Making a change that will be sent to
Bitucket using SSH
 1 file changed, 1 insertion(+)
 create mode 100644 README


$ git push
warning: push.default is unset; its implicit value is
changing in
Git 2.0 from 'matching' to 'simple'. To squelch this
message
and maintain the current behavior after the default
changes, use:

  git config --global push.default matching

To squelch this message and adopt the new behavior now,
use:

  git config --global push.default simple

When push.default is set to 'matching', git will push
local branches
to the remote branches that already exist with the same
name.

In Git 2.0, Git will default to the more conservative
'simple'
behavior, which only pushes the current branch to the
```

```
corresponding
remote branch that 'git pull' uses to update the current
branch.

See 'git help config' and search for 'push.default' for
further information.
(the 'simple' mode was introduced in Git 1.7.11. Use the
similar mode
'current' instead of 'simple' if you sometimes use older
versions of Git)

Warning: Permanently added the RSA host key for IP
address '131.103.20.168' to t
he list of known hosts.
Enter passphrase for key '/e/Users/Michael
Hanna/.ssh/id_rsa':
Connection closed by 131.103.20.168
fatal: Could not read from remote repository.

Please make sure you have the correct access rights
and the repository exists.
```

Don't be intimidated by the long warning message; this is just Git's latest version telling you that some of Git's default behavior will change in the future Git 2.0 release. Don't worry about that for now; you can avoid this message by explicitly typing

```
$ git push origin master
```

The more important issue is the line

```
Warning: Permanently added the RSA host key for IP
address '131.103.20.168' to t
he list of known hosts.
```

which tells us that Bitbucket has added our public SSH key to its list of known hosts. Unfortunately, I screwed up again and mistyped the passphrase, so the connection was closed with a fatal error. No worries, though; just try again. This time it works

```
$ !!
git push
warning: push.default is unset; its implicit value is
changing in
Git 2.0 from 'matching' to 'simple'. To squelch this
message
and maintain the current behavior after the default
changes, use:

   git config --global push.default matching

To squelch this message and adopt the new behavior now,
use:

   git config --global push.default simple

When push.default is set to 'matching', git will push
local branches
to the remote branches that already exist with the same
name.

In Git 2.0, Git will default to the more conservative
'simple'
behavior, which only pushes the current branch to the
corresponding
remote branch that 'git pull' uses to update the current
branch.

See 'git help config' and search for 'push.default' for
further information.
(the 'simple' mode was introduced in Git 1.7.11. Use the
similar mode
'current' instead of 'simple' if you sometimes use older
versions of Git)

Enter passphrase for key '/e/Users/Michael
Hanna/.ssh/id_rsa':
Counting objects: 6, done.
Delta compression using up to 4 threads.
```

```
Compressing objects: 100% (3/3), done.
Writing objects: 100% (3/3), 357 bytes | 0 bytes/s, done.
Total 3 (delta 1), reused 0 (delta 0)
To ssh://git@bitbucket.org/DarthVader/bash_project.git
   ade7eac..8307de9  master -> master
```

Eliminating Most Passphrases by Running ssh-agent

Unfortunately, even though we are now configured to use the SSH protocol to communicate with Bitbucket, we still have to enter the passphrase each time we try to update the repository. Let's add another file to our project and see what happens when we try to upload the change to Bitbucket:

```
$ cat > BYTEME
An unneeded file for our project.
<Ctrl-d>

$ git add BYTEME

$ git commit -m "See how SSH works a second time."
[master 437a2da] See how SSH works a second time.
 1 file changed, 1 insertion(+)
 create mode 100644 BYTEME
```

Before we attempt to push our update to Bitbucket, it is interesting to note that the 'git status' command is smart enough to know that our new commit has not yet been pushed to the main repository on Bitbucket:

```
$ git status
On branch master
Your branch is ahead of 'origin/master' by 1 commit.
  (use "git push" to publish your local commits)

nothing to commit, working directory clean
```

If you try to do the 'git push' command as usual, you will once again be prompted to enter your passphrase, which is *not* what we want:

```
$ git push
warning: push.default is unset; its implicit value is
```

```
changing in
Git 2.0 from 'matching' to 'simple'. To squelch this
message
and maintain the current behavior after the default
changes, use:

  git config --global push.default matching

To squelch this message and adopt the new behavior now,
use:

  git config --global push.default simple

When push.default is set to 'matching', git will push
local branches
to the remote branches that already exist with the same
name.

In Git 2.0, Git will default to the more conservative
'simple'
behavior, which only pushes the current branch to the
corresponding
remote branch that 'git pull' uses to update the current
branch.

See 'git help config' and search for 'push.default' for
further information.
(the 'simple' mode was introduced in Git 1.7.11. Use the
similar mode
'current' instead of 'simple' if you sometimes use older
versions of Git)

Enter passphrase for key '/e/Users/Michael
Hanna/.ssh/id_rsa':
```

In this case, *do not* enter the passphrase. Instead, type <Ctrl-c> to cancel the push. In order to eliminate the need to type the passphrase on every connection to Bitbucket, we need to run an additional program called 'ssh-agent,' which is included in your Git Bash installation.

The purpose of the program is to hold the private keys used for public key authentication. After ssh-agent is started, information that allows other processes to communicate with the agent is stored in two environment variables, $SSH_AUTH_SOCK and $SSH_AGENT_PID. The program does not initially store any private keys; they have to be added manually by running the 'ssh-add' program, which is also part of your Git installation. If a private key has a passphrase associated with it, you will be prompted to enter the passphrase when you add the key to ssh-agent. Once private keys have been added, you can see a list of fingerprints of the keys stored in ssh-agent with the command

```
$ ssh-add -l
```

Once ssh-agent has a private key stored in it, the SSH protocol will communicate with the agent any time it needs a private key. Since SSH can get the key directly from the agent program, you won't need to enter the passphrase after you have added the key to ssh-agent.

It is best to start ssh-agent and use ssh-add to add keys to it by executing code from your .bashrc file. There is some example code on GitHub that shows how to structure the commands needed to start ssh-agent:

```
https://help.github.com/articles/working-with-ssh-key-passphrases
```

The code is broken up into multiple Bash functions and commands that call those functions. Since the code is rather involved, I saved it into a separate file in my home directory, called ~/.ssh_agent_bash_functions. I then source this code from .bashrc by adding the following code to my .bashrc file:

```
#-----------------------------------------------------------------------
#  Start the ssh-agent process for communicating with remote repositories
#  without having to enter the passphrase more than once.
#-----------------------------------------------------------------------
function start_ssh_agent ()
{
  SSH_AGENT_FILE=~/.ssh_agent_bash_functions

  if [[ -s "$SSH_AGENT_FILE" ]]
  then
    echo "Sourcing $SSH_AGENT_FILE"
    source "$SSH_AGENT_FILE"
  fi
}

#-----------------------------------------------------------------------
#  Source functions needed to run ssh-agent. Note that this only needs to
```

```
# be done when you are communicating frequently with a remote repository
# and don't want to have to enter an SSH passphrase every time you
# connect. Whenever you aren't working on such a project, the line can be
# commented out. Note that functions need to be defined before they are
# used.
#------------------------------------------------------------------------

start_ssh_agent
```

Unfortunately, the sample code from GitHub is rather flawed, because it is heavily based on the assumption that there will only ever be one instance of ssh-agent running. If you have multiple Bash windows open and decide to experiment with the code, it is very easy to inadvertently start new instances of ssh-agent. And if you get rid of the newest ssh-agent process, you'll end up with a set of SSH environment variables that don't match the current instance of ssh-agent. The code wrongly assumes that 'ssh-add -l' will return a status of 2 if the agent is not running, but if the SSH environment variables don't match the agent process, 'ssh-add -l' will fail and return a status of 2 because it couldn't open the socket connection to ssh-agent using the value in $SSH_AUTH_SOCK. This explanation will probably sound like a bunch of mumbo-jumbo until you have experimented with the GitHub code, but the net result is that the code's agent_is_running() function can wrongly claim that the agent is *not* running when in fact it is.

If multiple ssh-agent functions are running, you will have to stop one of them. You can see which processes are running with the 'ps -ef' command (another useful GNU utility):

```
$ ps -ef
      UID        PID      PPID TTY         STIME COMMAND
Michael       5868         1 con        Mar 29 /usr/bin/sh
Michael       4416      5868 con        Mar 30 /c/Program Files
(X86)/Vim/vim74/gvim
Michael       7740      5868 con        Apr 14 /c/Program Files
(X86)/Vim/vim74/gvim
Michael       8792         1 con        Apr 17 /usr/bin/sh
Michael       3172         1   ?     11:55:23 /usr/bin/ssh-agent
Michael       2864      8792 con     02:51:34 /usr/bin/ps
```

You can also pipe it through grep to look only for the ssh-agent process:

```
$ ps -ef | grep ssh-agent
Michael       3172         1   ?     11:55:23 /usr/bin/ssh-agent
```

You can manually stop a process with the GNU 'kill' command. You have to tell it the process ID or PID that the ps command lists for that process. To kill the ssh-agent in the above example, you would type

```
$ kill 3172
```

I have made some improvements to the GitHub code, so hopefully you won't have to manually kill spurious ssh-agent processes. You'll notice that my agent_is_running() code doesn't use 'ssh-add -l' at all; instead, it looks directly at the list of processes and counts how many occurrences of ssh-agent are running. I believe this is a more reliable method of determining whether the agent is in fact running. Below is the full code for the ~/.ssh_agent_bash_functions file:

```
#       FILE:   .ssh_agent_bash_functions
#               -------------------------
#
#       This is a modified version of code taken from
#
# https://help.github.com/articles/working-with-ssh-key-passphrases
#
# which in turn came from
#
# http://superuser.com/questions/441854/git-ssh-agent-not-working
#
# This file should be sourced by .bashrc or copied wholesale into .bashrc.

# Note: ~/.ssh/environment should not be used, as it
#       already has a different purpose in SSH.

SSH_AGENT_ENV_FILE=~/.ssh/agent.env

# Note: Don't bother checking SSH_AGENT_PID. It's not used
#       by SSH itself, and it might even be incorrect
#       (for example, when using agent-forwarding over SSH).

agent_is_running()
{
    NUMBER_OF_AGENT_PROCESSES=$(ps -ef | egrep ssh-agent | wc -l)

    #  If ssh-agent is NOT running, return failure status

    if [[ $NUMBER_OF_AGENT_PROCESSES -eq 0 ]]
    then
      return 1

    #  If ssh-agent IS running, return success status
```

```
    elif [[ $NUMBER_OF_AGENT_PROCESSES -eq 1 ]]
    then
      return 0

    #  If more than one ssh-agent process is running, give up in disgust
    #  and let the user fix the mess manually.

    else
      echo "ERROR:  agent_is_running() detected more than 1 ssh-agent
process."
      echo "         This requires manual intervention to fix."
      exit 1
    fi
}

agent_has_keys()
{
    # if your keys are not stored in ~/.ssh/id_rsa.pub or
~/.ssh/id_dsa.pub,
    # you'll need to paste the proper path after ssh-add

    ssh-add -l >/dev/null 2>&1
}

agent_load_env()
{
    if [[ -s "$SSH_AGENT_ENV_FILE" ]]
    then
      . "$SSH_AGENT_ENV_FILE" >/dev/null
    else
      echo "ERROR:  agent_load_env() can't load nonexistent file $
{SSH_AGENT_ENV_FILE}"
      exit 1
    fi
}

agent_start()
{
    (umask 077; ssh-agent >"$SSH_AGENT_ENV_FILE")

    if [[ -s "$SSH_AGENT_ENV_FILE" ]]
    then
      . "$SSH_AGENT_ENV_FILE" >/dev/null
    else
      echo "ERROR:  agent_start() couldn't create file $
{SSH_AGENT_ENV_FILE}"
      exit 1
    fi
}

#  Convenience function to manually unset variables when things get messed
#  up.
```

```
unset_ssh_vars ()
{
  unset SSH_AGENT_PID
  unset SSH_AUTH_SOCK
  unset SSH_AGENT_ENV_FILE
}

#  This code should never have been included by GitHub, since the env file
#  won't exist until after ssh-agent is started for the first time.

#  if ! agent_is_running; then
#    #  agent_load_env
#  fi

# if your keys are not stored in ~/.ssh/id_rsa.pub or ~/.ssh/id_dsa.pub,
# you'll need to paste the proper path after ssh-add

if agent_is_running
then
    echo "Skipping start of ssh-agent since it is already running..."

    if [ ! "$SSH_AUTH_SOCK" ]
    then
      echo "Sourcing ssh-agent environment variables for this instance of
Bash..."
      agent_load_env
    fi
fi

if ! agent_is_running
then
    echo "The ssh-agent program is not currently running."
    echo -n "Do you wish to start it?  (You will need the password) (Y/N):
"

    read answer

    case "$answer" in
      [Yy]) echo "Starting ssh-agent..."
            if agent_start
          then
            ssh-add
          fi
          ;;
      [Nn]) ;;  #  Do nothing
          *) echo "Unknown option; ssh-agent not started."
          ;;
    esac
elif ! agent_has_keys
then
    ssh-add
```

```
fi

#  Don't unset this variable, since the user might need to manually call
#  agent_load_env() if the environment gets screwed up due to ssh-agent
#  inadvertently getting started multiple times while experimenting with
#  this code.

#  unset SSH_AGENT_ENV_FILE
```

Note that if you start the ssh-agent process you will need to enter your passphrase, so I included some code asking whether the user wants to start the process. If you forget your passphrase and need to look it up, just answer 'N' or 'n' to prevent the agent program from starting. After you find your passphrase, you can then re-source .bashrc or close your Bash window and re-open it.

Once you have saved this code to ~/.ssh_agent_bash_functions (and added the previous code to your .bashrc file to source this file), you should be able to do the command

```
$ source ~/.bashrc
```

in each open Bash window that you have. If you want to be on the safe side, close each Bash window and then re-open it. This will cause .bashrc to be automatically sourced. After your Bash windows are open, do 'ps -ef' to confirm that only one ssh-agent process is running. You can also do the command

```
$ env | egrep SSH
SSH_AGENT_PID=3172
SSH_AUTH_SOCK=/tmp/ssh-BfpgY10544/agent.10544
```

You should see that the value of $SSH_AGENT_PID matches the PID for ssh-agent that is shown by the 'ps -ef' command. When I sourced my .bashrc file (using my 'sb' alias), I was asked for the passphrase for my private SSH key when the ssh-agent program was started:

```
$ sb
Sourcing /e/Users/Michael Hanna/.ssh_agent_bash_functions
Starting ssh-agent...
Enter passphrase for /e/Users/Michael Hanna/.ssh/id_rsa:
Identity added: /e/Users/Michael Hanna/.ssh/id_rsa
(/e/Users/Michael Hanna/.ssh/
```

id_rsa)

After starting the agent, let's make a random change to the last file that we added and try pushing the change to BitBucket:

```
$ gvim BYTEME &

$ git add BYTEME

$ git commit -m "Made a random change"
[master 8192778] Made a random change
 1 file changed, 1 insertion(+)

$ git status
On branch master
Your branch is ahead of 'origin/master' by 1 commit.
  (use "git push" to publish your local commits)

nothing to commit, working directory clean

$ git push
warning: push.default is unset; its implicit value is
changing in
Git 2.0 from 'matching' to 'simple'. To squelch this
message
and maintain the current behavior after the default
changes, use:

  git config --global push.default matching

To squelch this message and adopt the new behavior now,
use:

  git config --global push.default simple

When push.default is set to 'matching', git will push
local branches
to the remote branches that already exist with the same
name.
```

```
In Git 2.0, Git will default to the more conservative
'simple'
behavior, which only pushes the current branch to the
corresponding
remote branch that 'git pull' uses to update the current
branch.

See 'git help config' and search for 'push.default' for
further information.
(the 'simple' mode was introduced in Git 1.7.11. Use the
similar mode
'current' instead of 'simple' if you sometimes use older
versions of Git)

Counting objects: 7, done.
Delta compression using up to 4 threads.
Compressing objects: 100% (3/3), done.
Writing objects: 100% (3/3), 329 bytes | 0 bytes/s, done.
Total 3 (delta 1), reused 0 (delta 0)
To ssh://git@bitbucket.org/DarthVader/bash_project.git
    437a2da..8192778  master -> master
```

The key output is the last several lines from the 'git push' command. You can see that our changes to the local repository were pushed to the main repository on Bitbucket without any need to enter our passhphrase again. As long as our Bash window is open and the ssh-agent program is running, we'll be able to communicate with Bitbucket without any need to manually enter passphrases.

That was kind of a long hairy mess, but if you made it this far, you should now be able to use Git to collaborate with others using a main repository hosted on Bitbucket. If you use a hosting service other than Bitbucket, the steps you need to take to get set up properly should be very similar. Your biggest stumbling block the first time through will probably be that of getting your public key copied properly to your remote repository.

Conclusion

If you read this book straight through and are new to Bash and its UNIX-style commands, your head is probably spinning. As long as your head doesn't actually detach from your body, you'll be okay. Once you have some practice with using Bash, you'll find that it is much more powerful than trying to work from a cmd.exe window. Bash's history commands alone, along with command-line completion and the ability to easily edit previous commands are already significant improvements over the traditional Windows command-line environment.

When you start using the included GNU utilities and begin to get comfortable with combining them via pipes and I/O redirection, you will begin to understand the real power that UNIX and Linux brought to the world.

Better yet, once you start using Git for source control, you will find that it becomes much easier to manage complex software projects.

Keep in mind that this book has only scratched the surface of even Bash itself. Bash includes many additional capabilities that we haven't discussed, as do the many utilities included with your Git installation. Even this brief introduction will go a long way toward helping you understand how a full-blown Linux system works. (Linux provides many additional utilities which will magnify your capabilities even more.) The philosophy of combining small programs with pipes and I/O redirection, and the ability to write scripts using any of these programs is what makes the UNIX/Linux model so powerful. This is why Linux powers a large percentage of the world's Web servers, despite Microsoft's dominance on the desktop. I hope you have enjoyed learning about where some of that power comes from. (And I hope you'll forgive me for ending the book the same way I started it: with a preposition at the end of a sentence!)

Appendix

Bash Reference Books

Albing Carl, Vossen JP, and Newham, Cameron. *Bash Cookbook: Solutions and Examples for Bash Users.* O'Reilly Media, 2007.

Newham, Cameron. *Learning the Bash Shell.* O'Reilly Media, 2005.

Robbins, Arnold. *Bash Pocket Reference.* O'Reilly Media, 2010.

Git Reference Books

Chacon, Scott. *Pro Git.* Apress, 2009.

Loeliger, Jon and McCullough, Matthew. *Version Control with Git: Powerful Tools and Techniques for Collaborative Software Development.* O'Reilly Media, 2012.

Silverman, Richard E. *Git Pocket Guide.* O'Reilly Media, 2013.

Bash Online References

A quick guide to writing scripts using the bash shell. http://www.panix.com/~elflord/unix/bash-tute.html (accessed 05/01/2014)

BASH Frequently Asked Questions. http://mywiki.wooledge.org/BashFAQ (accessed 05/01/2014)

Bash Quick Reference Card. https://code.google.com/p/linuxeden/downloads/detail?name=Bash_Quick_Reference.pdf (accessed 05/01/2014)

Bash Reference Manual. http://www.gnu.org/software/bash/manual/ (accessed

05/01/2014)

Cooper, Mendel. *Advanced Bash Scripting Guide.* http://tldp.org/LDP/abs/html/ (accessed 05/01/2014)

Garrels, Machtelt. *Bash Guide for Beginners.* http://tille.garrels.be/training/bash/ (accessed 05/01/2014)

Gite, Vivek G. *Linux Shell Scripting Tutorial v1.05r3 A Beginner's handbook.* http://www.freeos.com/guides/lsst/ (accessed 05/01/2014)

Wideling, Billy. *Alien's Bash Tutorial.* http://www.panix.com/~elflord/unix/bash-tute.html (accessed 05/01/2014)

Git Online References

Burgess, Andrew. *Easy Version Control with Git.* http://code.tutsplus.com/tutorials/easy-version-control-with-git--net-7449 (accessed 05/01/2014)

Chacon, Scott. *Pro Git.* http://git-scm.com/book (accessed 05/01/2014)

gittutorial(7) Manual Page. http://schacon.github.io/git/gittutorial.html (accessed 05/01/2014)

Git Cheat Sheet. http://cheat.errtheblog.com/s/git (accessed 05/01/2014)

Git Magic. http://www-cs-students.stanford.edu/~blynn/gitmagic/ (accessed 05/01/2014)

Meridth, Jason. *Git For Windows Developers - Git Series - Part 1.* http://lostechies.com/jasonmeridth/2009/06/01/git-for-windows-developers-git-series-part-1/ (accessed 05/01/2014)

Vanderplas, Jake. *Version control for fun and profit: the tool you didn't know you needed.* http://www.astro.washington.edu/users/vanderplas/Astr599/notebooks/07_GitIntro (accessed 05/01/2014)

Vogel, Lars. *Git - Tutorial.* http://www.vogella.com/tutorials/Git/article.html
(accessed 05/01/2014)

Acknowledgments

First, I would like to thank the many contributors to the open source community who have made Git, Bash, and the writing of this book possible.

I would also like to thank Trish Hartmann for graciously making her photographs available for public use under a Creative Commons 2.0 license. I used her "Florida Fighting Conch Shell" image for the cover of this book. If you appreciate the beauty of seashells as well as computer shells, you might be interested in Hartmann's book "Bivalve Seashells of Florida," which is available at

http://www.anadarapress.com/

This book was written using LibreOffice Writer Version 4.1.5.3. The fonts are the usual suspects: Times New Roman for the body text and top-level headings, along with Arial for secondary and tertiary headings. The one slightly unusual choice was to use DejaVu Sans Mono for the code examples rather than Courier New. Complete scripts are shown in boxed text, while code snippets are not boxed. No fancy typography here, but I hope you'll agree the results are at least readable.

The cover was created using Inkscape Version 0.48. Additional processing was done with the ImageMagick 6.8.9-3 Q16 x64 'convert' utility, and the file was converted to a PDF with LibreOffice Draw.

I apologize in advance for any errors that remain in this book due to my sloppy typing (or even sloppy thinking). You are welcome to report errors to me at the address

software_expert@sonic.net

The opinions expressed in this book are solely my own, and are entirely correct. ☺

Index

A

Acknowledgments, 229

Adding Files to the Staging Area/Index, 178

Aliases, 100

Alternate Consoles, 27

Ampersand, 42

Annotated tag, 182

Appendix, 225

Arguments to Commands, 47

B

Background job, 42

Backticks, 106

Bang bang, 39

Bare repository, 197

Basename, 122

BASH, 29

Bash Command History, 37

Bash Online References, 225

Bash Positional Parameters, 87

Bash Predefined Single-Character Variables, 87

Bash Reference Books, 225

Bash Variables, 86

Basic Bash I/O Redirection and Pipe Symbols, 81

Basic Branching, 185

Basic Git, 175

Basic Merging, 187

Bg, 43

Bitbucket, 196

Blobs, 178

Bourne-Again Shell, 29

Bram Moolenaar, 53, 136

Branch, 185

Break and Continue Statements, 122

Built-in Commands, 31

C

Caret, 55

Carriage return, 18

Case Statements, 115

Cat, 63

Cd, 31

Cd .., 61

Character classes, 54

Chmod, 111

Circumflex, 55

Clip, 206

Cmd.exe, 1, 104

Command Line Completion, 36

Command Options for the Less Utility, 65

Command Substitution, 105

Commit message, 179

Commit number, 183

Committing Files, 179

Conclusion, 223

ConEmu, 27

Configuring Bash with the .bashrc File, 106

Configuring Bitbucket to Use SSH Instead of HTTPS, 208

Configuring Global Commands, 176

Connecting to a Remote Repository Via SSH, 209

Console, 27

Cp, 62

CR, 18

Creating a Label, 182

Creating an SSH Configuration File, 205

Creating SSH Keys, 204

Ctrl-z, 42
Curl, 167
Cygwin, 7
D
Date, 105
Diff, 167
Directory Handling Commands, 34
Directory stack, 35
Dirs, 35
Docx2txt, 53, 71
DOS box, 1
E
Echo, 34, 112
Echo -n, 113
Editing and Sourcing the .bashrc File, 107
Egrep, 69, 70, 71
Eliminating Most Passphrases by Running ssh-agent, 213
Emacs, 38, 142
Emacs editing commands, 38
Env, 95
Environment variable, 93
Esac, 116
Exit, 104, 112
External command, 34
External commands, 31, 46, 50
F
Fg, 43
Fi, 116
File Comparison Tests, 118
File descriptors, 80
File Globbing, 54
File name expansion, 54
Find, 65
For Loops, 118
Foreground job, 42
G
Git, 6
Git Bash Properties, 24
Git Bash shell, 6

Git Bash Shortcut, 23
Git branch, 185
Git checkout, 185
Git clone, 192
Git diff, 189
Git init, 176
Git log, 183
Git merge, 187
Git Online References, 226
Git Reference Books, 225
Git remote, 193
Git show, 184
Git status, 177
Git tag, 182
Global variable, 93
GNU on Windows, 165
GNU readline library, 38
GNU Utilities, 49
GnuWin, 171
Graphical User Interface, 1
Grave accent, 106
Greedy, 78
Grep, 71
    Command Line Options for grep, 79
    Useful Options for grep, 79
Grouping and Negation for Tests, 116
GUI, 1
GVim, 9
H
Hidden Files, 47
History, 38
History Substitution Commands, 41
Home directory, 33
Hosting service, 196
I
I/O Redirection and Pipes, 80
IDE, 9
If statement, 113
    Condition, 113
    Formatting Notes, 3

What This Book is Not, 2
Who This Book is For, 2
If-Then-Else Statements, 112
Index, 178
Initializing a Repository, 176
Installing the Public Key into Bitbucket, 205
Integrated Development Environment, 9
Internal Field Separator, 121
Interprocess communication, 83

J
Job Control, 42
Job Control Commands, 44
Jq for Reading JSON Files, 173
JSON, 173

K
Kill, 217
Kill %job_number, 44

L
Label, 5
LAMP, 2
Larry Wall, 53, 71
Less, 64
Let statement, 126
LF, 18
Linefeed, 18
Linus Torvalds, 5
Local variables, 93
Local Versus Global Variables, 93
Long argument, 48
Looking at Information in the Repository, 182

M
Main line of descent, 187
Make file, 118
Man, 53
Master repository, 5
Merge conflict, 188
Merge conflict., 201
Miscellaneous Utilities, 173

Mkdir, 46, 58
More, 65
More Advanced Bash, 111
Multi-Character Regular Expressions, 74
Mv, 62

N
Newline, 18
Nl, 168
Notepad++, 146
Numeric Comparisons, 117

O
Od, 170
Other Shells, 104

P
Parameter substitution., 130
Parent directory, 32
Path Names with Spaces, 30
PID, 217
Pipe, 80, 83
Popd, 36
POSIX bracket expression, 78
POSIX Bracket Expressions, 75
    [:alnum:], 75
    [:alpha:], 75
    [:blank:], 75
    [:cntrl:], 75
    [:digit:], 75
    [:graph:], 75
    [:lower:], 75
    [:print:], 75
    [:punct:], 75
    [:space:], 75
    [:upper:], 75
    [:xdigit:], 75
PowerShell, 1
Powershell.exe, 104
Predefined Variables and Positional Parameters, 86
Process ID, 217
Prompt Variables, 92

$PS1, 92
$PS2, 92
$PS3, 92
$PS4, 92
Ps -ef, 216
Public key cryptography, 203
Pushd, 35
Pushing to and Pulling from Remote
Repositories, 198
Pwd, 31
R
Read, 113
Redirecting I/O for Loops, 132
Regular Expression Grouping and
Alternation, 74
Regular Expressions, 70
Remote, 193
Repeat a command, 39
Repository, 5
Richard Stallman, 50
Rm, 58
Rm -i, 60
Rmdir, 58
S
Sdiff, 167
Secure SHell, 203
Seq, 169
Set, 96
Setting a Default Editor, 180
Setting Sublime Text 2 as the Default
Editor, 181
Setting Up a Remote Repository, 195
Shebang line, 112
Shell Character Class Notation, 55
Shell File Globbing Wildcards, 54
Shell Functions, 102
Shift, 91
Short argument, 48
Short-circuit evaluation, 116
Single Character Regular Expressions, 74

Sort, 95
Source, 107
Special Characters for Word and Space
Matching, 76
\<, 76
\>, 76
\B, 76
\S, 76
\W, 76
Squiggle key, 33
SSH, 203
Ssh-add, 215
Ssh-agent, 214
Ssh-keygen, 204
Staging area, 178
Standard error, 80
Standard input, 80
Standard output, 80
Stderr, 80
Stdin, 80
Stdout, 80
Stephen Bourne, 29
Storing Variables, Aliases and Shell
Functions in .bashrc, 109
String Comparisons, 117
Subdirectory, 33
Sublime Text 2, 152
Subprocess, 93
Subshell, 93, 102
T
Tag, 182
Tee, 84
Testing Conditions, 116
Testing the Connection, 207
Text editor, 135
The Bash Programming Language, 111
The shift Builtin, 91
Tilde, 33
Tokenize, 54
Touch, 58

Type, 33
U
Unset, 95
Until Loops, 133
Unzip, 143
Using env and set to Look at Global and Local Variables, 95
Using Python from Git Bash, 161
Using Ruby from Git Bash, 159
Using set and shopt to Set and Unset Shell Options, 97
Using SSH to Connect to Remote Repositories, 203
Using the XAMPP LAMP Stack from Git Bash, 163
V
Variable interpolation, 94
Version, 5
Vi commands, 38
Vim, 9
Vim and GVim, 136
W
Wc, 83
Wget, 167
Where is the .bashrc File?, 106
While Loops, 125
Wildcard characters, 54
Windows Clipboard, 206

Windows drive partitions, 30
Word processor,, 135
Working directory, 178
Writing Scripts, 111
:
:gs/old/new/, 41
:s/old/new/', 40
!
!-2, 39
!!, 39
!?command_string?, 40
!command_number:, 39
!command_string, 40
.
.gitconfig, 176
\
\n, 18
\r, 18
&
&, 42
^
^old_string^new_string^, 40
~
~, 33
$
$IFS, 121
$PATH, 107

Made in the USA
Middletown, DE
21 February 2019